Education Ministry in the Congregation

Eight Ways We Learn from One Another

Education Ministry
in the
Congregation

Norma J. Everist

AUGSBURG Publishing House • Minneapolis

EDUCATION MINISTRY IN THE CONGREGATION

To my family, Burton, Mark, Joel, and Kirk, that primary teaching/learning unit which provides for my life, love, and continuity, and to the congregations I have been privileged to serve who have excited me with the reality of their being Christian learning communities.

I thank the students at Yale Divinity School and Wartburg Theological Seminary, who over the past seven years have trusted each other enough to try on these teaching and learning styles to see which ones fit their own emerging skills, and in so doing have deepened my own insights. I especially thank student assistants, Lowell Hennigs, Randell Fett, and Sandy Berg for their faithful participation and assistance.

Contents

Introduction

"Marge, I'm glad I caught you. You just have to help me out. Sunday school starts again in two weeks. We still need a sixth-grade teacher. I've asked everybody. You'll do it, won't you?"

Caught between swallows at the mid-August Sunday morning coffee hour, Marge gulps. What can she say? It's too late to hide. It's also too late to change her reputation as someone who accepts last-minute urgent requests. *I'd feel guilty if I said no,* she thinks. *We need enough teachers if we're going to have an active Sunday school. Enrollment is low enough already. But just once I'd like someone to ask me what I'd like to do in the Sunday school.*

"Oh, sure, Dave. When can you give me the books?" Marge mumbles.

This scenario is repeated over and over in rural and urban, young and old congregations throughout the land. There are variations, of course. In some congregations, the pastor, having desperately been asked by the super-intendent to use the authority of the pastor's office to find a last-minute teacher, will corner members of the church to persuade them to "use their gifts" to "help us out." Sometimes with an air of presumption, the pastor will thrust a teacher's manual and lesson booklet into the prospective teacher's hand, so as to seal the deal before the invitation is even made.

This is such an annual ritual in some congregations that come the middle of August, Marge instinctively avoids Dave. The pastor avoids the superintendent. And Dave, well, from whom can he hide? Feeling like an ogre much of the time, these education leaders, relieved when they sign up the full contingent of teachers, hide from them the rest of the year, lest one should ask to be replaced, thereby starting the recruitment process all over again.

Now, of course, not every Sunday school is plagued with such a desperate cycle. There is much joy in the educational wing of churches as year after year students and teachers alike, in substantial numbers, return to their classrooms. But for those for whom the middle-August syndrome is at least remotely familiar, the following chapters offer ways the congregation and the pastor can think together about the mutual ministry of education. This book is for pastors and congregation leaders in the area of education. Ultimately this book is for and about the whole congregation, because teaching and learning involves all of the people, whether they know it or not.

All too often, congregations, discouraged by dwindling class enrollments or their inability to entice teachers to come to training classes, seek new life outside the congregation. A new, colorful curriculum promises guaranteed student interest. And so, without careful examination, the congregation purchases "an end to all our problems." Other congregations, somewhat intimidated by the budgets and facilities of public schools, want to know what is the "latest." Not taking time to consider the unique task and opportunities of the church's educational ministry, they say, "That's what our children are receiving in public school. I guess that's what we should do too."

"What is the newest?" or "What will work?" may sound like good pragmatic appproaches to Christian education. But such statements are really symptoms of the difficulties in church-education programming.

Curriculum as God and God's people

The curriculum cannot be purchased! The curriculum is God and God's people gathered together at a certain place and time in history. All else is resource. A congregation has a life and mission of its own. The people are the primary resources. How are the people teaching and learning from one another?

Pastors and education leaders do well to sit down at least once a year to ask that question. Who are the people? How are they teaching each other? What are they learning from one another in the myriads of ways they interact, inside and outside of the classroom? What are the formal educational offerings for each age group? What learning takes place on other occasions when they gather, in choir rehearsals, church council meeetings? What are the people learning and teaching in the ways they care for each other, in the ways they worship, and in the way they live out the Christian life?

Such a survey often prompts an affirmation of God at work through Christian interaction. Such affirmation is sorely needed, particularly for the formal teachers often grown weary with what seems to them a lonely task. Reviewing and planning together are themselves encouraging activities, for they can help a congregation gain perspective and once again become excited together about the continuing opportunities to nurture one another in the faith.

Such assessment can provide opportunity for asking deeper questions. The ministry of education in the congregation is, after all, a theological as well as an educational endeavor. What are we teaching when we come together? Are we teaching that new life in Christ is a joy and a challenge? Are we teaching that it is dull and unrelated to life? Are we telling each other that we have a trustworthy or a tentative God? Does our educational ministry, in form as well as content, teach of a God of strength and care? Or are we, by the very doldrums into which we have descended, perpetuating a doctrine of the church which operates primarily on accommodation to guilt?

We need not be surprised that we from time to time become frustrated with ourselves as a teaching/learning community. We are frequently tempted to shortcut the gospel by running a guilt trip on one another, or by trying to fix up a class with a Band-Aid approach so it will hold together until the end of the year. If August and early September have their tense moments, what happens if we look in on Dick and Sue in February when flu season brings low attendance, when lessons seem boring even to the teacher, and when discipline seems dangerously absent? We do dare to take a February look, for it is into the midst of our most depressing teaching problems that God comes once more calling these people, this "curriculum" to be the people of God, together.

14

Setting the learning environment

God has given us to each other in Jesus Christ. Teaching, first of all, is creating the setting in which we can be present—really present— with one another. We need to set a learning environment in which teaching and learning can take place. Once that environment is established, a teacher can use any one of a number of teaching methods (as described in the rest of this book). Once the trust level is established, the students are able to be with one another. They are able to listen and learn and to create something together: some new understandings, new connections, new directions that could not have happened had these people not come together in this place at this time.

When this environment exists, a teacher and a class know it. You might recall such experiences, perhaps outside a formal classroom, from your own history of being a learner. This kind of learning environment lessens the number of times one hears a teacher say, "I can't get their attention," "I can't keep their attention." A teacher has the responsibility of erecting a disciplined situation with safe boundaries for people to bring their real selves to class. If we fail to create such a situation, the result is unclear expectations, inappropriate groupings or authority struggles in which discipline problems fester or inattentiveness and absenteeism are the norm. We set in motion a game which students—adults as well as children —eagerly play: "Please entertain me." We respond by "riding herd," enticing or begging the students to be students.

When we abdicate our responsibility of setting a learning environment, we look outside ourselves for the answers, and say, "Find me some lesson materials that will hold their interest." There are no such materials; even the most colorful and best written may eventually bore us. Even though this book is about teaching methods, there is no one method which will automatically cure discipline problems. We set a disciplined environment so that we can choose appropriate methods to meet the varying needs of students and the range of learning objectives. Once this disciplined environment is set, students are free to be really present, and all become engaged in maintaining the environment without games playing or power struggles. People can learn to be learners and to learn in community.

What are some charactertistics of a learning environment in which people are free to learn? It will be a place where there is safety for the self. Teachers will have given attention to place and pace, to people and to groupings, to mood as well as to the mind.

In order for a person to learn, the individual must be able to bring her whole self to class, not merely the proper or the "correct" self, but one who thinks, feels, and questions life, reality, and relationships. The learning environment needs to be a safe place to talk and to be and to feel—and therefore to grow. Such a class will be free of sarcasm, will invite the student to share failures and doubts as well as successes, and will respect confidentiality.

Such a learning space needs to be physically safe. Under the guise of being kind, some teachers permit students to endanger themselves and others. There should also be clear and helpful time boundaries. If the teacher is not present early, students will come later and later. Class members, of any age, can commit themselves to one another, knowing that each person and each person's time is valuable and valued by the others.

Place and time need to be appropriate to the learners;

noise, light, color, heat are variables that aid or hinder learning.

A good learning environment includes high expectations that something important is going to happen. How can we group people so that they can reach their potential? Besides the obvious age groupings, we might consider the way people learn—actively or quietly. We could group according to the level or depth of sharing desired. To learn creatively is to be able to learn at one's growing edge, neither bored nor fearfully frustrated. The students need to be free to know and to be known.

In a well-established learning environment the teacher does not need to worry constantly about keeping control. In a classroom where the teacher is always trying to gain control, but afraid to assert authority, the group is always on the verge of learning. When teachers and learners first establish a relationship in which they can be fully present to one another, neither will be undisciplined. The learners will be free to be all they can be, to use their minds to the fullest. The mood may change with the day. People may be quietly present with each other, struggle with one member, or joyfully excited with group discovery that spills over into activity outside the classroom.

Are such learning environments mere fantasies? No, they exist, in church basements, seminary classrooms, Christian homes. They are at the same time gifts of a gracious God and careful creations of dedicated teachers. They are worth our attention, for once created we can begin to teach and learn together using a wide variety of approaches.

Eight facets of learning

In this book wo will look at tho total picturc of cduca tional ministry from different perspectives. We categorize the variety of teaching/learning styles in eight ways, devoting a chapter to each facet of the fantastic gem of education. These chapters are not so much an attempt to acquaint people with new styles as a way to look systematically at educational ministry in its diversity, characterizing each facet by the direction of the flow of teaching/learning energy. Through looking at the parts of the whole we may better be able to design a balanced approach to our ministry of education.

1. Presentation
This facet of learning is characterized by presentation of the teacher to the learners. We examine how we learn from presentation of new material, giving attention to the two most common forms, lecture and storytelling, looking at ways to more effectively use this time-honored approach.

2. Worshiping community
This facet is characterized as multidirectional. In many and diverse ways people are learning from one another, merely by being the people of God together in a congregation. It examines models and mentors, as well as the congregation at worship. Also included are intergenerational learning and family cluster.

3. Discussion
This facet shows the flow of learning from the student to the teacher and other students. Although discussion takes place in every classroom and accompanies other

types of teaching, little attention has been given to the nature and effectiveness of discussion. How does one learn from putting ideas together and from verbalizing those new ideas? How can the teacher hinder or facilitate learning from the "inside out"?

4. Inductive study

This facet could be pictured as a continuum. One learns in the very act of learning how to learn some more. In order to develop to one's full potential as a learner, one must ask, know, speak, and do. Inductive learning is being led into these activities, which enable one to continue to discover for oneself. We give special attention in this chapter to inductive Bible study at different age levels.

5. Individualized learning

This facet of learning takes seriously the concept that people learn as individuals, even when grouped into classes. It is on the side opposite the facet of *worshiping community*. By looking at developments in British and U.S. schools, we will see how Christian congregations might be able to use these concepts.

6. Confrontation and clarification

This facet is pictured as people facing other people and other ideas—confronting and perhaps colliding. It examines the popularity of values clarification in the past two decades and seeks to see it in perspective. Also included in this chapter are testing, debate, and the learning possibilites of conflict in the congregation.

7. Experiential learning

Learning is characterized in motion in this facet. We look at drama, not as presentation, but with the learners as the actors. What are the presuppositions of such methodologies as simulation gaming, biblical simulation, role play, case study, and family sculpture? We shall look again at such familiar styles as the field trip and retreat and explore the learning possibilities in real and vicarious life experience.

8. Journal keeping

One could picture this facet of learning as having a time dimension. Present learning potential is the culmination of our life history of learning experiences. The journal, a tool for reflection and growth, facilitates learning from one's own life. How can the journal be a learning tool within the Christian community?

How to use this book

The book is written for people to read by themselves—as individualized learning. It also assumes that education is a ministry of all the people of God. Selected chapters could provide stimulus for discussion at meetings of Sunday school teachers and education committees.

Educational ministry deserves the very best thought and time priorities of the pastor. Rare is the congregation that has vital educational ministry, at least for any length of time, when the pastor is not actively engaged in open and affirming ways. This ministry of education formally involves many of the laity. Pastors who do engage directly and frequently with the lay teachers soon find such interaction stimulating, for people who are teaching want to be learners as well. In speaking with pastors and congregation educational leaders, I have found strikingly direct correlation between despair and lack of teachers' meetings, and a direct correlation between enthusiastic creativity and regular teacher-training and in-service events.

There can be a downward spiraling of problems: low attendance at teachers' meetings, bickering, blaming, lower attendance, and giving up. On the other hand, when a broad range of congregation members come together to talk and affirm and plan, work their plans, and then come together again to assess and gain perspective and dream some more, new directions emerge and enthusiasm is generated. If a congregation is not having teacher's meetings and has not had a congregation-wide planning session, it needs to take a leap of faith and try that very thing to which "no one will come."

The methods and illustrations from actual congregations are presented here to stimulate thinking about the teaching and learning which are happening in the reader's congregation. What are we teaching? What are we teaching by the *ways* we teach and learn from one another? Being a Christian teaching/learning community is an exciting, challenging venture.

Chapter 1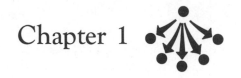

Presentation

As the storyteller describes an old woman, the hearer decides how tall or bent she will be. Do her eyes twinkle or stare? Is she bitter or hopeful? The learner's own world view may contribute to these decisions.

"And he began to speak to them in parables, 'A man planted a vineyard. . . .' " Jesus was a storyteller. That lost art has been rediscovered in the past few years. For many it was never lost.

"My favorite childhood Sunday school teacher was a marvelous storyteller. In fact, she's still telling stories to this day. Me? Well, I have to rely on the children taking turns reading the story from the workbook. How can I compete with the interesting things children see on television these days? I guess some of us are born to be storytellers and some of us not.

"By the way, I saw my old teacher just this morning. Her hair is white with just a touch of that chestnut brown

I remember as a child. Her walk is still as crisp as her words. As she came down the street toward me, I noticed she wore a worried expression. . . ."

This self-effacing Sunday school teacher, while denying her own gifts of story presentation, is engaged in it. All day long, wherever people encounter people, they hear and share stories, pieces of life that another has not experienced. And so, even when the workshops and books on "how to tell a story" pass again from popularity, the story will continue, wending its way down through history. In fact, in many ways one can say that the story *is* the down-through-history communication of human life, from one day to the next, from one generation to another.

Revelation and experience

As an educational style, the telling of a story, the presentation of information, has a theological presupposition. Every time one person speaks, acts, or shows a film to another, he is assuming that the audience or spectators have something to gain from receiving this new information. All there is to know is not already inside the human being. We need God's revelation. We need to receive God's revelation from other people.

Human beings are curious; we want to learn from others. We cannot always be experiencing, doing, or creating. We spend a good deal of time receiving information from one another. We vicariously experience what others have lived; from that we learn and grow.

That we can learn from someone's presenting something to us while we remain still, listening, watching is a gift. Imagine for a moment how skilled, capable, knowledgeable we would be if we were able to learn only through direct experience. What would be known? Would we know about the Russian revolution? What would we know about the moon? What would we know about our grandparents? What would we know about God?

Presentation or storytelling, is only one facet of learning. Indeed we could hear and read about God's activity in the lives of all the believers and know little about God's forgiveness and strength in our own lives. Our own experience of God is valid and crucial, but we know more about God through hearing about the human experience of God through the centuries. This provides a healthy safeguard against our own propensity to create the world in our own image. God's creating us to learning vicariously enables us to know God more clearly. Even then, human experience of God through the centuries is not all there is to God. God is beyond God's own revelation.

Vicarious experience through listening to a lecture or a story complements our own experience. Learning through being spectator or audience is an enjoyable way to learn. Are we able to learn well through presentation? Are we active or passive when hearing a story? How can we help people learn how to learn through story and lecture?

Efficiency and inefficiency of presentation

Studies have shown that we remember 10% of what we read, 20% of what we hear, 30% of what we see, 50% of what we hear and see, 70% of what we say ourselves, and 90% of what we say and do. Viewing these figures, we might conclude that presentation is rather inefficient. It is!

On the other hand, presentation often makes the most efficient use of time. Hearing someone describe their trip to Ethiopia or seeing slides of that trip is much more expedient than going there ourselves. The effectiveness of the speaker, the quality of the slides, as well as our own ability to learn vicariously determines how much we will "know" what living in Ethiopia is like, or at least what visiting in Ethiopia is like.

What then are the effective methods of presentation that help another learn well? One might be tempted to believe that if simple clear telling is good, then telling with pictures and music is even better, and so on until one reaches the height of excellent dramatic presentation. The fact that excellent dramatic presentation is available at the flick of the dial has intimidated teachers. How can our little drama be good, or good for the student? We wonder. We're afraid no one will hear the message for the flaws. But one need only remember Meredith Wilson's *Music Man* to recall that we receive even the most sour note and think the music grand when we care about the person who is playing the trombone for us.

This is not to condone or encourage mediocrity, but merely to lower our level of intimidation. Four elements are essential to the effectiveness of presentation as a teaching methodology: 1) caring about the people with whom we are sharing and not being afraid to let it show; 2) caring about the material we are going to share, knowing it so well and wanting others to know it so much that we *must* share it; 3) selecting a method of presentation which is well within our repertoire and making proper preparation; and 4) doing it well.

1. Caring about the learner

No matter how colorful our description or how amusing the anecdote, if we do not love the people to whom we are speaking, that fact will overshadow the excellence. Some people use humor to try to establish rapport, but humor can distance the speaker, if its goal is to make the audi-

26

ence think how funny we are. Any device we use to encourage others to think we are amusing, intelligent, and talented may have the desired effect, but it may not teach anything or help the learners feel more curious or competent.

If we care about the learners, we will select material that we know they need to hear, not just that which will make us look good. If we care about the learners, we will tell our story or deliver our lecture in such a way that the hearers know we are thinking about them. If we care about the learners, we will select material that we know they need to hear, not that which will make us appear as a marvelous performer. We will have specific learner goals in mind.

2. Caring about the content

Recently a person recounted the joy still felt because a college instructor was so excited about history. "This may sound strange, but we couldn't wait to come to class; because he was so excited about European history, we were excited too."

The Christian faith comes alive for students when the teacher's own belief is strong. Such a teacher does not need to demand allegiance on the part of the students. An intense, lively presentation will communicate that the teacher believes in what she is teaching. Such faith is caught by the student.

Being honest about our own doubts is equally important. Saying we don't know the answer to a question is appropriate. In recent years, however, in reaction to the role of knowing everything perfectly, some teachers have begun to teach in such a low-key way that the student is left with a flat impression of the subject. A passion for what we teach, blended with compassion for the student, provides a powerful learning experience that will be long remembered.

3. Selecting the appropriate style

One of the most effective, and therefore memorable, representations of the annunciation I have witnessed was a simple reading of Luke 1:26-38 at the beginning of an Advent service. An adult woman, a newcomer to the congregation, and of a different background from most of the other members, was dressed simply in a costume suggesting she was portraying Mary. After the opening hymn, she walked to the chancel and stood quietly, in a posture of receptivity and awe. Another woman, a good reader, simply read the section from Luke. Allowing some time for the people to receive the words and to ponder them, the two then returned to their seats, and the service continued.

The material was not new, but the words came to us as new and communicated two things: 1) Christmas is not just for children, nor is a Christmas pageant a time for children to dress up and look cute for their parents; 2) Christ comes to us in the midst of the world, through people we might not expect to be God's messengers. Mary was a plain, simple, unknown person, hardly the one we might expect God to choose.

We choose a style of presentation that is within our capabilities, that is congruent with the message, and that can be understood and received by our audience. We should resist the urge to copy a TV production or the performance of a larger church. The church choirs I have heard painfully performing something beyond their training have caused more discomfort than joy. Likewise, I have heard a presentation by a choir of five which reached me and touched me because they rejoiced in the gifted

28

people they were and in simple fashion sang music appropriate to their gifts.

This does not mean that we should at all times do the easiest and simplest; stretching ourselves to new use of our talents is also important. Many times I have been deeply moved by a lecture, a story, a play in which people had high expectations of themselves. An example is a play in black light performed by a company of mentally retarded adults for a convention of religious educators in Canada. It was excellent, for they selected the appropriate medium and gave the best of themselves.

4. Doing it well

The method we choose must be used well. Even though stretching ourselves to new use of our talents is important, we must be confident of our competence and the competence of those whom we ask to participate. Lack of either makes our audience uncomfortable or embarrassed, and the message is lost.

We do not need to strive for perfection, for that often communicates an insecurity or more concern for the production than the people. But the medium we select should be carefully chosen and prepared and done well. Presentation of God by one person to others, when done in love of the people and in love and commitment to the content of the material, is indeed a gift. The learner will receive it in the mode in which it is given.

Storytelling

There are many methods of presentation, but in this chapter we shall focus primarily on two that are most frequently used in educational ministry—storytelling and lecture.

To some, storytelling is fantasy, pretense, entertainment, the opposite of truth and real life. On the contrary, the telling of the story of God and God's people is real. Storytelling is a rich way to bring that real story to us who live in a real world.

"Once upon a time" begins many a fairy tale. Fairy tales have their place. In *The Uses of Enchantment* Bruno Bettelheim says that as children wrestle with myth and fairy stories, they answer the question "What is the world like?" and work out inner struggles of good and evil.

But good and evil exist externally as well as internally. The biblical story is not only to help children work out internal struggles. The story of God and God's people is true *outside* of our existence and also true *for* our existence. The truth about God and God's people in another time is relevant, perhaps the only relevant truth, for living in this time.

Keeping this tension is important. Many people today talk about the biblical story becoming "my story." In storytelling, we identify with certain characters. But we can do that with any story, and, in fact, do. (Ask your class about their favorite TV shows and which figures they identify with.)

We are related to the biblical story more directly than through "identification." We have already become part of God's story, by God's action, in our Baptism. God called us, united us with God's people of all history. Because of that reality we now want to learn the story and become acquainted with our brothers and sisters in the faith.

How the story becomes ours

There are many books on the art of storytelling.[1] This book will not duplicate those, but will examine what happens to learners who hear the story.

When we as educators tell a story, we often do too much. The more the learner is engaged in painting the picture the better. (Listening to a radio story was more of a participatory act than listening to and watching TV.) We need not add an explanation to the story, a moral. If the story will not stand by itself, then it is not a good story or is not well told. If the students will not grasp the meaning of the story, our telling them *what* to understand will not make them understand any better. The listeners will either be insulted or disrupted from their own inductive learning process.

A young woman preached a fine sermon about the biblical story of the woman at the well; she simply told the story. We saw the woman, we thirsted for water. We struggled and were embarrassed with Christ's questions. We anticipated the displeasure of the disciples, mentally left the water jar, and rushed with joy to the city. We understood the story. We understood more clearly our own sin, the remarkable knowing nature of God and the caring grace of our Redeemer.

That is enough. To do more is to add some "shoulds" and "oughts." If in our story the learner comes to think about sin and sin's resulting problems, we have accomplished an important objective. If in the story the learner hears God's forgiveness proclaimed and Christ's healing manifested, another essential objective is accomplished. We must trust that the Spirit readies the hearts of the learners to appropriate that message for themselves. Once we add words which dictate *what* the person should conclude or should feel, we have placed the learner back under the law. By the Spirit's guidance, when they are yet hearing the story, they, like the woman at the well, know that their sin is five times worse than first mentioned. If the law and the gospel have been presented

31

clearly in the story, Christ already will have been present through the story and will have announced in the hearts of the hearers the words we have spoken from the biblical story, "I who speak to you am he."

The story lives

When a story is told with clarity and awe, what happens within the learner? Different stories begin to grow in the minds of each hearer. How exciting it would be to peer into the mind's eye to see the technicolor productions taking shape, each with individual meaning for that individual! The picture formed depends on the past experiences of the hearer as well as the descriptive ability of the storyteller. As the storyteller describes an old woman, the hearer decides how tall or bent she will be. Do her eyes twinkle or stare? Is she bitter or hopeful? The learner's own world view may contribute to those decisions.

The story session may be over, but the learners continue to carry that story with them. One person may repeat the story to parent or friend, emphasizing points significant for him or her. Another may move on to a myraid of other thoughts, although the story is stored in the mind and may be brought to consciousness again. The story becomes intermingled with life experience and relationships, facts and attitudes, and becomes a part of the person who hears it.

Learners are likewise affected by the many stories they hear during the week. Our mind does not separate the secular from the sacred. How many stories has each of us heard this very day? Our child told us about an incident at school. A neighbor phoned to relate a story about a sick friend. A partner at work told of a frightening episode on vacation. A spouse just had to tell about a meeting last night and the resulting hard feelings in the group.

Having told the story, the spouse can now go about today's work. But the story lives on in the listener, perhaps "teaching" something, with or without that being the goal of the storyteller. The listener draws the conclusion that some individuals with that group last night are unjust and unfair. If the "learner" has occassion to meet those people, attitudes and actions will have been influenced.

The teachers in a Christian congregation include everyone, for everyone is a storyteller. We do well to listen to the storytelling that is a part of the daily lives of our members. What stories are being told? What stories are being heard? What are people learning?

For such a time as this

Although many believe youngsters are the primary audience, storytelling is for all ages. Adults enjoy a well-told narrative. Although insulted by cute little stories in workbooks, teenagers too can learn from appropriate use of a story.

Recently a group of eighth graders were studying the wisdom and story material of the Old Testament. They were unfamiliar with the story of Esther and the origin of the Festival of Purim. What better way to present Hebrew story literature than through story? So, on a snowy January evening the nine young people pulled their chairs in close, not to be distracted by others in the large fellowship hall.

With Bible on my lap I proceeded, "In the days when the Hebrew people. . . ." As we reached the part of the story where Esther was faced with the decision of whether to deny her heritage or go before the king and risk death, one boy, who had also opened his Bible, interspersed, "I bet she was afraid, and with good reason. It says here the king had already done away with one queen."

They delighted that the plotting Haman was himself done in and cheered that Esther had accepted the challenge of Mordecai, "Who knows whether you have not come to the kingdom for such a time as this?" They eagerly listened to the end and heard that the Festival of Purim is still celebrated today. They saw how God's people had once again been saved from annihilation. They also saw the subtleties and alternatives: "Queen Esther was not only brave, she also used her wits; she could have become a wealthy insider, but she remembered the people who were still outsiders."

We do well to discern if story is appropriate for a particular age level, for such a time as this.

Ways to increase story effectiveness

As we engage in storytelling as an art, there are many ways to increase our effectiveness. Perhaps the first is to be unafraid to put ourselves into what we are doing. A halfhearted storyteller embarrasses the group. A storyteller who hides behind a book, eyes down, concentrating on proper pronunciation of words, communicates little.

A storyteller needs to think about the story and have the outline and many of the details in mind so that he can become engaged with the learners. If the storyteller finds the author's words so delightful that they cannot be ignored, he may choose to read the story, being familiar enough with the content to establish eye contact with the hearers.

Some readers may well remember such storyreading in kindergarten and first grade. The fourth-grade teacher read less frequently, and the eighth-grade teacher who reads to the class is rare. The print is now small, and

34

there are few pictures. Why is it we believe that picture books are for children? Many times I have pulled Dr. Seuss' *The Sneetches and Other Stories* from my shelf to read to an adult class. Sometimes there is a piece of literature that says what needs to be said better than we ever could.

New storytellers, insecure in their art, sometimes glue themselves to a chair. That's rarely necessary, unless we have gathered little ones on our lap. Random bodily movement is distracting, but intentional movement enhances the effect of the words.

As we sit at a table with a class, we can use our hands. "Early in the morning the women went to the tomb." Our fingers move across the table and the eyes of the learners follow, actually seeing Mary Magdalene, Mary, and the mother of James and Salome. Our other hand is the door of the tomb. With our voice and the simple suggestion of our hands we express their surprise, "They looked and saw the stone was rolled away and the tomb was open!"

While standing, one can walk a step or two, adding to gestures and facial expression the mere suggestion of the story movement. The word of caution here is "subtlety." Overdone antics confuse and distract.

Sometimes the learners themselves can become props in the story. While speaking about ministry in the inner city, I have introduced hearers to this world, quite foreign to some of them, by describing the people who lived on our block. I told them brief stories of each household. Moving around the group, I fixed the buildings visually by attaching them to the hearers, as though they were the green house, the white house next door, the brick building at the corner. "As we come up tho other side of the street, in the two-family building, Mrs. Washington lives downstairs, taking care of her grandson, Anthony. She's a strong woman who recalls days of field work as a child. . . ." The story is made vivid through simple identification with the physical presence of the hearers in *their* world.

Methods of story presentation

One can add to the dramatic effect of storytelling by simple staging, with one person being narrator and another being a still-life actor. Likewise the amount of costuming and props is less important than the learning objective. A simple headband, a shepherd's staff, or a newspaper may be all the visuals needed.

In Chapter 7 we will explore the value of involving the learners as participants in the dramatic presentations. For now we confine ourselves to the varieties of ways the teacher is teller and the learners are receivers.

There are a variety of ways to tell the story. One could use special settings—another place in the church building or the out-of-doors. The storyteller could put the story on cassette, perhaps including sound effects. One class could become the storytellers for another class, presenting "reader's theater," with simple props.

An overhead projector is useful in storytelling. Common objects such as paper clips or buttons can be used to represent characters. Lay these objects on the projector "stage" and tell the story. Cut-paper shapes also work well on an overhead projector. Shadow boxes, story line, diagrams, flannelgraph—all present simple, but effective ways of in-classroom visualization in storytelling.

Many churches have their own slide projector and movie projector. Some have their own video equipment. Teachers may think these media are too difficult, but it may be only a question of having the equipment available, in good condition, with teachers briefed on how to use it. One resource person could aid the teachers in making full use of film and video.

If good equipment is not already owned, churches might consider going together to purchase equipment. The resource person will want to check out sources such as local libraries, schools, and cable access.

Films that are not specifically religious may have a great deal more potential than we think. Video taping a series of advertisements or clips from current TV shows could provide a presentation with unlimited potential for theological reflection. This is using the day-to-day material of people's lives. The films they see and the programs they watch are forming and shaping them.

The movie *Evan's Corner* has many possibilities. My husband has used it with children and adults, inner-city and upper-income suburbia. He simply asks at the conclusion of the film, "What did you see?" A little boy lives with his eight-member family in a two-room apartment. Evan wants some place in this apartment for his own. His mother says he might have one corner (after all, there are eight corners in the two rooms). He proceeds for the rest of the film to dream and work and fix up his corner. Finally, after we have seen the transformation, he decides something is still wrong. The final scene shows his new delight in wanting to help his brother have a place, a corner, of his own.

A simple story, but in it is potential for reflection about identity and community, stewardship, love, independence and interdependence, ownership and offering. The story itself is open-ended. It stands alone. The Christian child or adult will find meaning, perhaps more meaning than the writer or teacher intended. One person from a suburb said of the film, "That's us in the film," caring so much about fixing up our piece of property, when it is in reaching out that we really find joy.

We have moved from storytelling and presentation to reflecting on what happens within the learner. Storytelling is never just the craft of the storyteller. It also becomes a craft of the learner. The story is a significant part of teaching and learning, and probably will remain so. Once the learning environment is set, the story is set free. More things begin to happen than we might imagine.

Lecture

Although often maligned, lecture remains a prime method in teaching. The word has derogatory connotations. "Don't lecture me!" meaning "Your comments are judgmental." "It sounded like a lecture," means, "It was dry, boring, pedantic, irrelevant." But lecture can be a valid, vibrant learning style.

Problems with the lecture

However, lecture often is ineffective. Here are five problems with lecture:

1. *Lecture is used by people who believe lecture is the only teaching style.* Because this is the belief of lecture-oriented people, lecture is overused. When lecture is overused, we produce dependent learners, people who passively accept the lecturer's view as right and their own thoughts as wrong or uninformed. We quiet people in order that they might hear and learn, and then we do not know how to help them once again think and talk and write and create. With overuse of lecture we teach people that learning is sitting quietly, listening and taking notes. They learn to be passive.

2. *Lecture is used in predictable ways.* Students and teachers alike grow to expect 50 minutes of presentation, starting "where we left off" and going a predictable distance down the road. The style of the lecturer, the tone of the voice, varies little. Students come to expect no surprises and actually to resent them. Such predictable learning is comfortable.

3. *Once turned on, lecturers don't know how to turn themselves off again.* Anyone who has been a lecturer knows how compelling lecture becomes. As we become involved in the dynamics of the subject, as we hear our own voice, our mind becomes engaged. We are becoming more excited, our speech more facile; meanwhile, our listeners are dulled in their skills. When a student asks a question, we lecture for another ten minutes. The student, easily satisfied or unable to formulate a complex logical system on the spot, quickly becomes quiet again.

4. *Lecture provides only one point of view.* Even though we have selected from and synthesized varied resources, we have probably put together a clear statement of issues. This is understandable, for merely giving a series of sentences joined by "on the other hand" says nothing. The real cutting edge of learning takes place when students are exposed to a variety of ideas (See Chapter 6 on "Debate and Confrontation").

5. *Lecture engages only the ears of the learner.* Lecture provides additional resources for learning when combined with writing on a chalkboard or with use of the overhead projector or with handout sheets or outlines for students to take notes. Nevertheless, the students still feel compelled to place their own learning within the framework

of the teacher's outline. Even when making comments in response, the students feel they must shape them in the form of questions for the lecturer to answer, therefore at least somewhat negating the students' own creative thought and contribution. The learning environment needs safe boundaries, but not merely the structured boundaries of the teacher's outline.

Basic guidelines for the lecture

With all of the above shortcomings, lecture is still a valuable learning style that takes seriously the fact that we as learners need new ideas and outside information in order for us to become learned enough to create further ideas. Some basic guidelines may help:

1. *The purpose of the lecture is to inform.* Words are the fastest way to do this. One can use lecture to introduce, to explain, to compare, to summarize. For older elementary children, youth, and adults, reading is an even more efficient way to obtain information. But a teacher can bring information together in new ways for this particular group of learners, can adapt, make relevant, and combine information in ways that the printed page cannot.

2. *The lecturer should assume that the learners want to hear.* Caring about the students and caring passionately about the materials will be communicated. Some lecturers feel they must tell some jokes to hold students' attention, but the careful preparation and genuine desire and ability to share it will probably carry the lecture—even without jokes. Clarity, vivid examples, summarization are ab-

solutely necessary so that this difficult bridge from one person's mind to another's may be completed.

A lecturer who assumes students will sit quietly through anything, however, is fooling himself. I still recall classmates who during a junior college history course, routinely got up to pull down the shades so they could snooze. The professor never lifted his eyes, continuing to drone on, reading from his yellowed notes. Contrastingly, I recall three-hour warm summer school sessions. The professor, using only his voice, daily held us spellbound with stories of American church history. His enthusiasm was catching. We were eager to adapt the material and teach others in our own church settings.

3. *A lecturer needs to use the very best grammar, diction, and vocabulary she can possibly develop.* Body movement should add to rather than detract from the voice. Can you remember a junior high teacher who would stand for 10 minutes, then sit on the edge of his desk, then straighten his pants leg, then. . . . But what was he saying? Johnny Carson's nervous mannerism of straightening his tie may have become his trademark, but ours usually draw attention away from what we are saying.

If we are going to lecture, we should do it well. No need to apologize for using lecture as a teaching style if we are honing our skills, developing our vocabulary, polishing our descriptive expression.

4. *Lecture is for people.* One sometimes sees a lecturer reading a prepared speech rapidly. Glancing at his watch, then back to the paper, he picks up his place as though "doing" the paper were the goal. To whom was he giving the paper? His dialog with watch and lecture did not include looking at his audience. Were they fatigued?

Were they eager to respond? Had they gone home for lunch? Would the speaker have noticed? Where were they? Did he care?

Lecture, properly used, at every age level

When used appropriately, lecture can be effective with any age level. In a congregation's educational ministry program we often give the teacher who likes to lecture the adult class. Adults then miss the exciting challenge of experiencing more involving styles of learning. On the other hand, overreaction to strictly cognitive presentation has brought us in the past two decades to allowing children only to make collages or toothpick crosses. They have missed receiving new material, new ideas which can efficiently be presented through lecture.

1. *Young children.* Story is not the only palatable way for young children to receive biblical material. Here are budding conversationalists. Their vocabulary, though limited, is developing at the fastest possible rate. They figure out meanings from context and welcome new words and ideas.

The attention span of young children is short, but they, unlike adults, will let the teacher know when they can take it no more. Lecture which is filled with "you mustn't" and "you should" soon takes on the derogatory meaning. Brief, concrete minilectures, however, are appropriate for young children. They want to know about the world around them. They want to hear what the teacher has to say to them.

2. *For elementary school children.* Formal lecture may seem pedanic. Yet, lecture, defined as presenting informa-

tion in succinct, interesting relative ways, is useful, even with lower elementary age. Upper elementary children, 9-12 years old, are industrious, fascinated with language, new ideas, broader horizons, and particularly with facts. Their capacity to learn, on a subject with which they are intrigued, can seem limitless. One need never fall into the medicinal use of lecture, "this-is-for-your-own-good" talk. Rather, combined with other methods, ten-minute presentations of new material will be well received.

3. *For teens.* Junior high youth, like their preschool counterparts, will show with their whole beings they are not with you. *"Borrrring!"* is the cry. In order to work with junior-high age, one needs to set the learning environment and set it well. Once that is established, however, junior highs will be as likely to learn from brief lecture as from other methods. They might appreciate a refreshing, clear presentation in vocabulary which respects them. They like straight talk from a person they trust.

In preparing a curriculum for an eighth-grade class on world religions, I selected materials which used an experimental approach. We would become familiar with Hinduism by making Hindu foods. We would learn Jewish customs and talk about Hanukkah while we were carving *dreydels.* The students resisted. What was the nature of their displeasure? Their resistance said they actually preferred a straight informative approach. We shifted gears and approached the material factually, with significant amounts of lecture presentation. Only later, after they had received introductory material were they ready to taste Hindu food.

High school youth are able to deal with abstractions. Lecture is one method of teaching which can be unabashedly deep and intriguing. They may indeed respect a teacher who respects their ability to handle mature ideas. High school students in the church are no longer willing to merely sit and endure lecture. Most are no longer "taken" to church and Bible class but have some decision in whether or not they attend the high school class. A teacher at this level dare not lecture to merely pass the hour, but the high school age Christians do want the teacher to wrestle with concepts and to help them do the same. It is a time of questioning the faith which has been theirs primarily through affiliation with their family and the family of their church. They will either do their questioning inside the church or outside its walls. Balanced with other involving methods, lecture could provide wide enough boundaries to test out a broader range of ideas while still in the community of faith.

4. *For adults.* Adults have learned well how to learn from lecture, or at least how to sit passively and take in someone else's ideas. Lecture, therefore, should be used sparingly, or at least thoughtfully with adults. What is going on inside those still, straight human beings in rows in front of the teacher? They may actually prefer lecture, for it is not as risky as the more experimental methods to be described later in this book. Lecture does have the potential for presenting to adults in the church ideas that they do not ordinarily consider in the course of their daily lives. The goal is not to perpetuate passive learning, but to use lecture in combination with discussion and confrontational styles so that the total educational experience is stretching and challenging. Adults can talk about these very things and decide together how much lecture and what other styles would be helpful to them.

Though much maligned, overused and abused, lecture is

a basic educational ministry style. It is to be selected, not merely used because it is that to which we and the learners are accustomed. Good use of presentation, whether it be story, lecture, or any of the myriads of other forms, is marked by a teacher's passion for what he shares and compassion for his students. After the learning environment has been set, students are ready to receive new ideas, new stories from outside themselves, from outside their own community, from a transcendent God.

Presentation never stands alone as a teaching/learning style. When well done, it is a significant part of teaching, but it is only one facet of educational ministry.

Chapter 2

Worshiping Community

Joel could tell that Mrs. Greiman loved children, including him. When she went to the hospital, Joel sent her a card; Mrs. Greiman wrote back. . . . They are special to each other to this day, because she was special for him at that important age of four.

"We don't have any adult study groups," a pastor said. "In fact our church has become so small that we have only four Sunday school classes. I guess you could say we really don't have an educational ministry program here—at least nothing to speak about."

Even when a congregation has a small formal education program, much teaching and learning happens. There is no way we can stop education from happening in the Christian congregation. The question is not whether or not we are educating one another, but in what ways and to what end we are teaching one another.

Whenever two or three are gathered in the name of Christ, the Teacher is in the midst. We who have been

47

crucified with Christ have been raised to new life. Once we were no people; now we are God's people. We are a holy people, a people set apart. The Spirit is at work bringing forth the fruits of this new life.

What do those biblical images have to do with the education program of the congregation? Either we believe that Christian education is primarily information to be communicated, or we can take the deeper view that because we are God's people, something unique has happened and is happening to us. Is God at work in this motley crew? Yes. Among these very ordinary, often recalcitrant people, God has created and is creating a Christian learning community.

We who are God's people are continually growing and changing. We either grow or we die. The New Testament is full of imagery of vine and branches, of the fig tree, of the seeds and the harvest. Either Christians, attached securely to the vine, grow and produce fruits, or they wither and die.

One cannot count the number of adult learners in a congregation by adding up the people who attend formal classes. Someone may not have been in a class for years, but that person has continued to interact with the world and has continued to be formed and shaped by other Christians in the congregation. The question is, who and what is shaping and forming us? How are we being nurtured? What fruit are we bearing? From whom are we learning and whom are we teaching? How and what are we teaching by the very fact that we are part of the body of Christ and therefore connected with all the other members?

For years secular educators have written that the most formative influence on the child is the home and family. Likewise, the living together within the broader community of God's people has significant formative influence. The quality of relationships, the sense of purpose, the language and behavior powerfully educate the young person in the church. Into adulthood we continue to influence one another, in greater ways than we might imagine.

It is appropriate that Christian educators give attention to this important facet of learning, the Christian community itself, the people of God whose lives are centered around the worship of God. We can look at the body of Christ, in this place, and see if it is growing in healthy ways.

Each model in this chapter might be described as people learning from watching others, hearing others, and being formed in Christian living through being with one another. Generally this facet of learning takes place over some length of time. It is often intergenerational. Formation takes place within the nuclear family but grows in richness and strength when many outside the immediate family are involved.

We include in this chapter models and mentors. We also look at the gathered community, particularly in worship, but also in all of its activities together. We look at the diversity of gifts and ways of actualizing those gifts. Included also are family cluster and intergenerational learning, the more formal educational structures of this facet.

Models and mentors

Recent literature has revitalized the term *mentor*. Public educational material speaks about "modeling." The church, for years, talked about adults being "good examples" for young people. The terms are similar but distinct in possibilities.

Congregations may actually shy away from seriously considering the teaching possibilities in the ways a community lives together, because "good example" is such a "bad example" of teaching. At its best we were legalistically trying to produce people who could act in certain socially accepted ways. At its worst we were hypocritical and set people up for disillusionment and disappointment with Christianity.

"Good teacher," said the rich young man "What must I do to inherit eternal life?" "No one is good—except God alone," Jesus replies, fully aware that the young man considers himself good enough to stand before the rabbi and before God. When Jesus reminds him of the Commandments, the young man replies, "Teacher, all those I have kept since I was a boy." Christ adds, "One thing you lack. Go, sell everything you have and give to the poor. . . . Then come, follow me" (Mark 10:17-21).

When one is caught in the trap of being good for God, one must be good enough. How often we still teach "be good" in Sunday school, with the implication that it is possible and that we will grow up to be good example teachers in the world! Merely trying to be a nice person makes religion tolerable. Christianity is neat-as-a-pin when it is reduced to looking for and becoming good examples.

Followers of Christ, people on the way

But the open-endedness of "give to the poor" and "follow me" is not safe and not predictable. God provides for people a multitude of ways to know God's will. God gives people the minds and talents to become gifted people, wrestling with the complexities of human life and acting on them, and to follow Christ wherever that may lead.

The good example Christian is too careful to really walk and too limited to really see. Teaching people to follow Christ is open-ended and frightening, but an exciting adventure. It is not simple, neat, carefully controlled teaching.

Later in Mark 10 Jesus encounters another person, a man who could see nothing but, knowing he was a beggar before God, called out "Son of David, have mercy on me!" Jesus calls to blind Bartimaeus and restores his sight. "Go your way," Jesus says, and Bartimaeus follows Jesus. He now looks at life in a new way. In the looking is all the difference.

In that looking for mercy and following Christ within the Christian community, people become images of brokenness and the light of wholeness to each other. Such teachers and learners no longer need to pretend to be good, so they teach so much more. They look to each other because Christ is in the brother and the sister. They can learn from one another because a brother or sister in Christ has already walked the way before.

The book of Acts talks about people of the Way. All of Christ's disciples are "on the way," not to becoming good examples, but on the way in living in the world, already redeemed, struggling with problems of ministering in the world. We learn through Christians who are teaching us, whether they know it or not, through their lives. They have suffered and sinned, been redeemed and now rejoice. It is not their good-example lives, but their strength and courageous witness in the world which teaches, more powerfully.

Models are discovered, not appointed

In the 1980s in North America survival is a global issue, but, for many, not a personal daily question. Many young people today have not survived a struggle which produces courage, and yet they know about nuclear war, cancer, and a multitude of other life-threatening possibilities. The resulting despair has produced a high suicide rate among teenagers in the United States.

"I don't think I could stand being paralyzed for life; I would rather die," a high school student said after visiting a hospitalized friend. But the friend lives. The high school student learns vicariously the courage to live in the midst of problems in a dangerous world. The grace to grow is imaged for us by those whom the Lord has sustained, a wise elder, or even by a peer or a child.

How does one find such models? We might look back into our own lives and see whose face comes to mind. Who has already been a Christian saint in my life? Who has cared more about me than about what I have learned, thereby teaching me so much more than I could have imagined? Whose mannerisms have I mimicked? Whose ways have become my own? Whose values do I now live? Who have been the significant Christian people—the teachers—in my life?

Models are discovered, not appointed. Being aware of those teachers encourages us to look around and enjoy the discovery. Because we know that sound education ministry is happening through and among Christians in the congregation, we can accept the role of model when it is thrust on us by another.

A group of church women began discussing this facet of learning. I saw a surprised, yet pleased look on the women's faces as they began to think, "I have been a special Christian to another person. This is good. It is not a lack of humility to acknowledge how God is teaching—even through me."

We have many models in the faith. Parents are their children's earliest models. This important role may frighten people. We as a church might do well to encourage parents to build from the strengths they already have. The Lord has grown adults into perfectly able models for infants. In this confidence parents will be open to further learning, rather than abandoning their role in fear. As parents we continue to learn through seeing both effective and self-defeating ways of raising children. Older parents model, positively and negatively, for us.

About the age of four children select models for themselves outside the family. Some boys and girls become enthralled with the garbage collector, a person of the world, able to come and go, responsibly carrying out duties at regular intervals, able to swing those cans around and drive large trucks. Not strange that many a child has announced that he or she would like to become a garbage collector some day.

This is also a time to find a special person outside the family. For many children it is the kindergarten teacher. For our Joel it was Mrs. Greiman. She was not his Sunday school teacher, but a loving woman in the congregation. Joel could tell Mrs. Greiman loved children, including him. When she went to the hospital, Joel sent her a card; Mrs. Greiman wrote back. They enjoyed seeing one another each Sunday. The times we visited each other's homes were special. Joel and Mrs. Greiman are special to each other to this day, because she was special to him at that important age of four.

For our youngest, Kirk, another member of the congregation, Mrs. Pavia, played an important role. He frequently visited her home and when we moved far away sent school pictures once a year.

For Mark, our eldest, the college students who lived in our home in Detroit on weekends were special, fun, exciting, interesting. They sparked his interest in many subjects. He became a lively reader, fascinated with history and current events.

For teenagers, parents who have been models for years and whose influence will never really end, now seem to be the source of embarrassment. Teenagers need to think of themselves as other than the children of mom and dad. This is precisely the time that special adults in the Christian congregation can play such an important role, certainly for children from one-parent homes, but for all teenagers.

For years I sat in worship with the teenagers of others while they held my babies. Now as my own sons choose their colleges and vocations I pray that the ones who influence them at just that precise choice-making moment will be people of faith and worthy of my children's trust.

We continue to model and to discover models. Young adults with unsure commitment, watch marriages which have lived out that commitment for 40 or 50 years. Middle-aged adults look in hope or despair to the years ahead. The Christian who has succeeded and failed, but who trusts in God and has attained an inner sense of Christian hope and peace, is a powerful teacher for someone in the middle years. How important for the Christian community to consider the teaching and learning which happens in the models we have become for one another.

A mentor to guide and encourage

Selecting a mentor is a different matter because there is an intentionality in the choice. We look for unique qualities in a mentor and need a mentor more at certain stages of life. David Levinson in *Seasons of a Man's Life* and Gail Sheehey in *Passages* speak of the young-adult stage in which we look for someone a bit more experienced to guide us through those early career years. The trying twenties is a time to find a mentor, if possible. "She became my tutor," or "He took me under his wing," are ways people speak about that person from whom we learn in significant ways as we shape the vision of our own possibilities in the world.

In a mentor we see a person who is living a fruitful life. We seek wisdom from that mentor as we develop skills for our own life's work. When reflecting on mentors in their own lives, young adults have reported that not only is the mentor someone whom they admire, but the mentor also admires the "learner" and is willing to say that he or she sees potential in the young person.

In this unique teacher/learner relationship, the learner actually sees himself or herself in the mentor, at least for a few months or a few years. Gradually we may outgrow a need for our mentor, but that relationship of learning, so appropriate at crucial growing times, remains a special gift. The relationship itself often develops into a peer relationship.

A good deal has been written about men finding mentors; until recently little has been written about women, partly because in this society to be young and beautiful was more highly prized than to be a wise, perhaps wrinkled, woman of age. But as role stereotypes change, there are many new possibilities for this unique learning time, for women and women mentors as well.

The person learning from a mentor, whether it is formal, or more likely, an informal teaching arrangement, might ask, "What skills of living and serving in the world do I want to develop?" Admiration for a mature Christian is not sufficient, for in trying to copy the mentor's style we may disown our own gifts. Just as the good example can blind us, so admiration invites us to live only in the shadow of another. Mentors do well to guard against the ego satisfactions of keeping the young person dependent on the mentor. The wise teacher, says Kahlil Gibran, "does not bid you enter the house of his wisdom, but rather leads you to the threshhold of your own mind."

We continue to seek and become models and mentors for one another. In so doing, we witness the human condition and God's new life in Christ. Blessed indeed is that congregation where people can live among one another over the years, sharing in this educational ministry to one another and seeing each other develop in the life of faith.

The gathered community: the congregation at worship

Whether we spend a lifetime or a few brief months in one congregation, our attitude toward that collection of people will determine whether or not it can become a learning community for us. We could spend our days complaining about the congregation where we worship and never see the potential that is there. God has gifted us with the community in the place where we are. Trusting that, we begin to become acquainted with the unknown brothers and sisters in the faith. As we gather for worship, we all confess and receive absolution, becoming naked and reborn before God and before one another. Our life together is to actualize that which God has brought together and created whole. The question is not, "Will I like them?" "Will I allow myself to know and be known?" "Will I participate?" God has joined and knit us together in the body, and this is where we will grow.

This facet of educational ministry is centered in worship; we are created a people of God around the altar. In the one baptismal font we are reminded that we are united in Baptism to become a new, holy people. As we hear the Word, we become an empowered people, strengthened to live. As we eat the one bread and drink the one cup, we become the body of Christ for service in the world.

Why, then, do we sit in church seeing only the backs of each other's heads? Lest we hurry to redesign our sanctuaries, we are reminded that the pew arrangement is only symbolic of the problem, the spectator or audience mode of congregational worship. There are many problems, but also many solutions that can enhance the educational possibilities of the community at worship.

A few years ago we attended a festive service at a church in Manhattan. We were out-of-town visitors, and therefore strangers. We had small children along and were seated three-quarters of the way back in the church. The service was long; the children were restless. I was anything but involved, and I felt left out. Why such a feeling? The music was fine. The liturgy and preaching were fine. But I suddenly felt as though the people in the chancel were having "all the fun." Although worship is not for human amusement, we have been redeemed to enjoy God forever, to be united, not divided, from God and God's people.

In contrast to this experience was my attendance at a wedding in the Bronx a few years later. With the joyful, if crowded, comings and goings in the chancel, warm human involvement permeating the rich, formal liturgy, I had the feeling *everyone* was up in front. That feeling can happen every Sunday.

The two examples which I used were from churches where I was a visitor. Visitors or newcomers in a church are impressionable. What does our congregation at worship teach people the very moment they arrive? That people are here to worship God, or merely to inform others of an upcoming committee meeting? That we belong together or that this is an exclusive club? That the gospel brings joy and excitement, or that it is cold and judgmental? What does the church bulletin or worship folder teach? What do the symbols, the stained glass, the stones say? What does the mood of worship convey? How can we affirm or change this powerful teacher, the congregation at worship?

Children in worship

In some congregations the ushers seem to have been schooled in handing out church bulletins. They can adroitly slip them to incoming worshipers, in half a second flat, skipping everyone who is under four-and-a-half feet tall. A worship bulletin is helpful for a child. With it in hand she knows she belongs. Even a small child can look at the cover picture or symbol, while the young reader will try to follow the service. Children are believers too.

From the time he was six, our youngest worshiped in the front pew by himself unless the church was crowded and others had to take a front seat. He knew where the psalms, hymns, and liturgy were to be found and he worshiped well, using the bulletin to the fullest. If he did not have one, he would march to the door to find one.

The child who can *see* what is going on will learn much from being part of a congregation at worship. Infants and children should be in the front, not the back pews.

People use much "logic" to justify children not being in worship. "They cannot understand the words," they say. But who of us adults can understand fully the mysteries of God? "They cannot read the words to sing the hymns." Who of us concentrates fully on the words of each stanza as we sing? "A child's attention span is very short." Those who have faithfully brought their children to worship since birth have found that a child learns to remain relatively quiet in a relatively confined space.

Children should not, of course, be allowed to cry or talk so that others cannot hear. Early in my own motherhood I was told by an older mother, "I learned to take my child out when he was distressed, and then to bring him back in again." The child who is kept out will soon discover the doughnuts in the fellowship hall a good enough reason to fuss again next Sunday. Children who are brought back to worship are usually distressed less and less often.

The child learns postures of praise. Most important, the child learns that here are some people doing something important. They are serious and joyful at the same time. They say things which they seem to mean. They include me and make me feel as though I, too, belong among them, in this important place, doing significant things.

The words come soon enough. "Amen," the 18-month-old says at home. The three-year-old plays "Communion" with playmates, family members, teddy bear, and rabbit. Play is repetition of important ideas and acts. The child is repeating and rehearsing the roles of worship.

In churches where services last two or three hours parents seem to have little trouble with children in worship, perhaps because many allow the children to comfortably be a part of the wider community of adults. The younger mother who is tired from parenting alone all week will quickly become irritated when the child won't be quiet in worship. Why not share the care of this child with an older parishioner who longs for the days when his grandchildren were young enough to sit on his lap? It is not a mark of failure that we "can't handle" our children in church (unless that "good example" mode is still bothering us). It is a mark of community that we consider all the children in the Christian congregation our own. Is not that what we confessed and promised in the baptismal service?

In one congregation children eagerly sit with pencil in hand ready to listen to the readings and the sermon. They have heard the pastor say, "Children, listen to these words, and draw a picture of what they mean to you. You older children, write poetry about the ideas you hear." Afterwards these creative works are hung on a bulletin board under the title, "The Gospel According to Children."

Like models and mentors, the worshiping community teaches through formation, over an extended period. Sometimes adults say, "I didn't get anything out of the services this morning," as though they were there merely to learn and to take. This facet of learning takes seriously the fact that being together in the presence of the living God is an end in itself. We are there not merely to learn in a narrow sense of receiving some good ideas. We are there to repent, and to receive forgiveness, to praise and to petition, to sing and to share. Because we have been actors in this most important of dramas, not merely spectators or an audience, our lives are significantly changed. This is power-filled learning.

A false division: child learners, adult worshipers

Through their Sunday morning scheduling some congregations communicate that they believe that worship is for adults and education is for children. This false division has led to all kinds of misconceptions, such as the belief that adults need ministry while children need to be taught. All of God's people are able to worship and need to continue to learn. Children also need pastoral care, and adults need education. In addition, all can minister and all can teach—even, and perhaps especially, the child.

Some congregations have taken time to look at their total Sunday morning program. The design of time and space carry through the philosophy that they begin the morning together in worship and then go apart to learn, coming back together at the end of the morning to celebrate and share before going forth again into the world.

A congregation which I served took such a look at itself and then developed a similar schedule for Sunday morning. The adults and children had grown quite apart. Simply having everyone together in the sanctuary to begin the morning was a visual change. Children were welcomed to the front. New classes were begun for teens and adults. At the end of the morning all once again gathered in the sanctuary to share what had happened while they had been in separate classes. Children came into the adult class, literally took the hands of the adults, and gathered them into a large circle for closing sharing and prayer time.

Many congregations have instituted the children's sermon, which indeed can have value if not merely a "cute" show for adults, at the expense of the children. But this, too, can isolate the service into "times for children" and "times for adults." Actually the entire service is for all. A whisper of explanation about the liturgy or a word of encouragement to the young worshiper is hardly distracting.

When our eldest child, never sedentary, was two, we worshiped Sundays in a university chapel where between 1000 and 2000 people would come forward for Communion. We taught him to watch for people he knew for whom he might pray. "God bless Edie." He delighted in his skill of spotting a familiar face. And who can say that God did not use the blessings of this child for Edie or Marliss or Karl?

As they worship, adults and children will learn through thoughtful attention to the themes of liturgy and through adults and children participating in special ways—writing prayers, leading the chanting or speaking of the Psalm, adding visuals to hymns. Over the course of the years, a brief sentence or two introducing the scripture lessons teaches much Bible history. The words of the liturgy take on new meaning as they are highlighted according to the season of the church year.

In our congregation, once a year, on Maundy Thursday, we used a "narrative Communion" in the mode of the Passover question, "What is it we do this night?" Far from saying "We had that last year," people looked forward to this opportunity to hear the recitation of the meaning of the words and movement of the liturgy once each year.

A pastor in inner-city Chicago told a group of us visiting her parish, "Every Sunday must be special. There can be no plain, run-of-the-mill, it's just-another-Sunday service, for someone might come for the first time, or the last, this very Sunday."

Powerful teacher: disunity or community

There sometimes seems to be a gremlin present or perhaps it is Satan himself—which tells people they are not needed in worship, that they are much more needed in the kitchen to watch the pats of butter and the pickles lest they run away before the potluck dinner following church. Even ushers find reason to slip out of church.

Granted there are times that emergencies call people

from worship. Christ healed on the Sabbath. And in our day, we've had a flooded basement, sick children, a church fire, robberies, death, even a murder. But somehow such devastating reminders of the problems among us drew us closer together as we prayed and sang and heard the Word more clearly.

But that is quite different. The worshiping community which knows it is the body of Christ will realize all are needed in worship in order for the body to be whole. Only by faith do we perceive that we are members of one another, being shaped and formed by the Spirit. I have seen congregations where people believe the worship service belongs to the pastor, the Sunday school belongs to the superintendent, the women's guild belongs to Mrs. Brown, the usher's post to Mr. Smith. Each has her or his own little niche, and beware to anyone who treads on their territory! We can hardly be nourishing one another in such an atmosphere, yet our sinful nature may lead us in that direction.

If *disunity* is *community* gone astray, we need to recall that the things which called people away from their brothers and sisters into a self-protective position are often those things for which people have been given responsibility. The congregation that desires to become a teaching/learning/worshiping church must build in that direction. The one who has only been allowed to guard the door or the butter will do that well. Could not more people be engaged in attending to the physical needs of worship and the welcoming, having whole families usher together? Family, roommates, teenage groups can take turns writing the prayer. The ushers might have some important things to teach if they were invited to the educational program of the church. The women's guild as well as the Sunday school, could put on a pageant, not just on Christmas but any time.

At my ordination I was intent that we not reinforce old images of men serving the Lord's meal and women serving the other meal *after* the liturgy. After preparation and explanation, everyone attended the festive celebration and everyone brought food and served one another at the reception, concluding hours later with some of us vacuuming the floor in stocking feet.

The congregation that believes educational ministry begins and culminates in worshiping together will be able to go forth to serve. They will already have learned much about God and each other, about the truth of the faith memorized through singing and speaking again and again. They will have learned to pray from seeing one another pray. They will have learned that even when suffering and death are real, the resurrection is real, too. The family whose mother died yesterday is strengthened within the community this morning.

They will have learned that people with cancer may indeed be in pain and depression, but they are not without hope, for they sit beside us in the pew and teach others a strength in the Lord that is of ultimate value. They will have learned by speaking and hearing, by kneeling, and by standing to share the peace of the Lord.

Intergenerational learning and family cluster

Graded classes will continue to be the style of most congregations. Even with such homogeneous groupings for an hour a week, much intergenerational learning takes place informally. And an educational ministry committee can build on ways to learn new skills from one another. Is the congregation learning new ways to care for each other, taking a meal to a family with a newborn, offering to stay with the elderly when their primary caregiver is away? Are there ways to help people learn to listen to one another? Is the congregation growing and learning new ways to be effective change agents in the world? All these skills can be learned intergenerationally and through existing gatherings and groupings of people as well as through special times together, focusing on a task or a project, such as a mission fair or a refugee sponsorship.

Some congregations, however, have also formed classes in which children, youth, and adults of various life stages are present. Planning for such a class is not as difficult as it might seem if one emphasizes experiential learning activities (see Chapter 7) rather than on a cognitive method or lecture/discussion. Some discussion, of course, is useful to help people listen and learn from a person at another stage of life than their own.

A church might plan a certain amount of time, a few weeks or a summer session, in which to group intergenerationally, carefully selecting people, not from the same family, making sure that each group of 8-10 people has as broad a representation as possible. Materials can be found from curriculum resources which emphasize retreats. Family materials from vacation church school programs have appropriate intergenerational learning activities. The key is to create the learning environment where all feel of equal importance.

This will take more than words, for youth who talk easily with one another will often clam up or sit in the back when "dropped" into an adult class. The beginning activity needs to be one in which all are equally expert, such as sharing their earliest remembrance of being in a church. Once the learning environment of trust and openness is set, the group might be able to handle almost any topic.

There is a significant difference between grouping people intergenerationally, across family lines, and creating clusters of families. Misunderstandings result when, for example, a family retreat includes some families with young children and some couples who came to engage in adult activities and be away from children for a while. The word *family*, even with constant redefining to include "one or more persons who live in a household," still has connotations of exclusiveness to those who see a society geared toward the "typical" family, even though statistics show there really is not such a "typical" family anymore. Intergenerational groupings, cutting across family groupings, are by their very nature inclusive.

There are, however, important learning objectives that can be met by groupings of families. The dynamics which make families close can also block our interacting. Sometimes our attempts to speak the gospel to family members sound hypocritical because the loved one knows our faults so well. But when one's family learns together in the presence of other families, there is a measure of objectivity introduced.

Family-cluster learning is a way of supporting and building on the strengths already present in families. In recent years we have formalized most learning to the point that many families wonder just what—if anything—they can do well. The family has forgotten that it can teach one another how to play, and so there are courses at the Y and in the schools and summer parks and recreation programs that teach one to swim, play ball, do crafts. The family has forgotten that its members can teach one another to cook, to mend, to repair, to build, for we believe there are experts in the community whose skills outshine our own. The Christian family has forgotten that it can and does teach its members how to love, to care, to speak the faith, to forgive, to be responsive and responsible in the world.

Family clusters are one way of rediscovering the learning, caring unit that each family is. Watching another family share in devotions, listen, and laugh, can encourage my own as we try once again to do these simple, yet difficult, nurturing activities together.

God's gift of community

How can the congregation be the body of Christ and therefore nurture one another in continuous ways? First of all, by realizing that community is a gift; it is nothing we create. Dietrich Bonhoeffer wrote:

> Innumerable times a whole Christian community has broken down because it had sprung from a wish dream. The serious Christian, set down for the first time in a Christian community, is likely to bring with him a very definite idea of what Christian life together should be and try to realize it. But God's grace speedily shatters such dreams. Just as surely as God desires to lead us to a knowledge of genuine Christian fellowship, so surely must we be overwhelmed by a great disillusionment with others, with Christians in general, and, if we are fortunate, with ourselves. By sheer grace, God will not permit us to live even for a brief period in a dream world. He does not abandon us to those rapturous experiences and lofty moods that come over us like a dream. God is not a God of the emotions but the God of truth. Only that fellowship which faces such disillusionment, with all its unhappy and ugly aspects, begins to be what it should be in God's sight, begins to grasp in faith the promise that is given to it.[1]

The Christian community has been given a unique learning environment, one created new every day, with forgiveness, with new life, with new possibilities for living together and serving Christ in the world. We begin by giving thanks for it, for this is the people of God in the place where I am. This is a gift. We worship our God together and receive the multitude of ways God provides for us to grow through teaching and learning from one another.

Chapter 3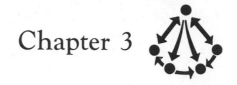

Discussion

If listening had been a competitive sport, I could have been a superstar. I'd probably have played in the world series and won the car. I listened to win. No matter what anyone said to me, I topped it.

A group of teachers, sharing which teaching style they preferred, responded, almost in unison, "Discussion!"

"That's when things come alive and everyone learns," one said.

Another added, "I really like discussion, but lately I'm having a hard time with my class. I can't seem to hold their attention. When I work on finding an interesting topic, they aren't interested at all."

A third teacher, comforted by the fact that someone else was able to admit difficulties, declared, "My adult Bible class sort of ended after Easter. Adults are simply too busy these days to discuss the Bible."

Boredom and absenteeism are seen as *class problems*. Actually they may be signs that people are not really engaged in their own learning. Teachers who know what lively discussion is seem hard pressed to know why a group, once buzzing with alert participants, suddenly seems embarrassed with the silence when a topic dies. In fact, this silence of dying discussion soon turns into a shuffling of feet, a watching of the clock. Adults start talking committee business. Children poke each other.

Why do some class discussions come alive while others never seem to begin? Why can't students become interested in a "perfectly good lesson"? Is the topic not challenging or are people with their silence saying, "That's not where I am; I have not yet claimed this subject as my own"? Once people are present with each other, bringing their whole selves along, an environment will be set in which people are able to be relevant. They are free to begin to think and talk where they are, and it will be safe to move into thinking with another.

Despite the large part it plays in the classroom, discussion has usually been ignored as a subject of discussion itself. Perhaps that is because many teachers consider discussion to be that which happens after the "real" lesson. "Students do the lesson (hear the story, read the page, do the work sheet), and then we can all discuss it." Even in college seminars, students will furiously take notes on the professor's lecture, then settle back and lay down the pencil when the real teaching/learning between and among people in the classroom is just beginning. How often do you see someone take notes on what a class member has said? Rarely, even though that may be the most significant contribution of the day.

Measured by what a person recalls and relates a day later, discussion may have been the core of class content.

70

Ask another student, "What did I miss yesterday?" and the student usually tells the subject of the class and then goes into some detail on one aspect of the discussion. And it is most often a contribution he himself made! Discussion is a valuable learning style because it invites the learner to claim a concept, think about it, create and shape a new thought, and put it into words. That shaped, spoken thought is the student's and he remembers it.

In this chapter we shall look at the art of discussion, giving attention to theological aspects, to being present with each other, and to some problems with discussion. We shall ask if every discussion, including questioning, is really beneficial to learners. We shall also look at Effectiveness Training, with its roadblocks and communication facilitators.

Chapter 1 dealt with the theological assumption that we have something to learn from that which is outside the self. Storytelling and lecture are therefore valid educational styles. This chapter looks at the opposite facet of this complex jewel of education, focusing on what is already inside the learner, waiting to be focused and spoken. The teaching tool in this facet is listening, listening well enough to find out what is about to be learned by the student's own verbalization.

God created people, not puppets

God has created people, not puppets, and our educational ministry should do no less. The potential for human development is immense. Few of us know the limits of our capacities. As children grow in the ability to think, act, and reason, they go through a developmental sequence. The children gradually become aware of a world outside themselves and learn how to relate to that world. They are not doll-like playthings, but human beings, valued by their Creator. As Christian educators we assert the dignity of the human individual and delight in discovering with that person as she learns.

Our view of the human person informs our teaching assumptions. A teacher who assumes the student is a sinner, unable to see or act in a holy way, will set about the task of conversion. The teacher who believes the child is in need of information in order to learn how to act will try to impart ideas and modify the child's behavior so that she will behave in Christian ways. Another teacher determines that the child needs to discover her own potential and values and then choose to live accordingly. Each of these approaches disregards part of the reality of the Christian learner.

The first two teachers will not value discussion as an important method. But the latter may ignore the basic human problem, a propensity to try to recreate the world in our image and manipulate others for our advantage. To teach as though a Christian student is always in error and in need of conversion or information, to straighten her out so the student knows more and acts better, is to ignore the person's Baptism and to play God. But we also come to false conclusions, even using the best of developmental theory, if we believe human beings will grow out of their problems. To use a learning style which encourages the self to emerge is extremely important, if kept in balance with the Christian awareness that at every point we continue to sin and need God's forgiveness.

Kohlberg's theory of moral development

Lawrence Kohlberg's important work has helped educators realize that one must take seriously the level of development of the student, that person's ability to understand, to discuss, to respond. Kohlberg identifies six stages of moral development, two stages occurring at three distinct levels, the preconventional, the conventional and the postconventional:

Preconventional level
The child responds to rules and labels good and bad, but interprets these labels in terms of physical consequences or in terms of power of the one who gives those rules.

Stage 1: Punishment and obedience orientation
Physical consequences determine right and wrong, regardless of human meaning or value. One simply avoids punishment.

Stage 2: Instrumental exchange orientation
Right is simply that which satisfies one's own needs and occasionally the needs of others.

Conventional level
The person is loyal to, maintains, and supports the expectations of family, group, or nation, regardless of immediate personal consequences, but without perceiving the value of ideas in their own right.

Stage 3: Mutual interpersonal orientation
One learns approval by being "nice." Good behavior is that which pleases others and is approved by them.

Stage 4: Law and order orientation
Right behavior is doing one's duty, maintaining the social order according to the authority.

Postconventional autonomous or principled level

A person tries to define moral values apart from the authority or identification with authority.

Stage 5: Social contract orientation

Right action is defined in terms of general rights and standards which have been critically examined and agreed upon.

Stage 6: Universal ethical principle orientation

Right is defined by abstract, ethical principles—universal principles of justice, respect, human rights.

There is no set age at which an individual crosses from one stage to the next, but research has shown that each person does proceed through these levels in this sequence. Some adults do not go beyond the third or fourth stage, whereas the Constitution of the United States is a Stage 5 document.

In a Christian class we may be trying to discuss the meaning of Christian freedom which enables one to serve the poor, assuming a Stage 5 orientation. A student at Stage 3 may be agreeing with the teacher in order to gain approval or, a person at Stage 4 may want the teacher to provide a set of guidelines or new rules to help the poor "as the church says." A person may behave at one level and be able to comprehend discussion at one level higher, but will not be able really to understand a stage two or more above his level of behavior. Discussion, real discussion, is challenging because of developmental differences.

At every point the developmental pattern must be seen from the perspective of sin and grace. As we grow more able to engage in abstract reasoning, reaching higher levels of moral development, we continue to need Christ's forgiveness for we likewise develop more subtle ways to deny God, to deceive ourselves, and to destroy each other. Some of us even manage to do so in rather "mature" ways.

How do we deal with developmental systems and Christian theology? And how does this question bear on the educational style that begins with what is inside the human person? We learn all we can about human development—physical, cognitive, emotional—for God has created people who grow, not puppets. We do not merely pour in information, or try to straighten out behavior, ignoring how the person is perceiving reality. At the same time we do not take a strictly humanistic view, for the inner self and outward behavior do not only need maturation, but forgiveness.

Within the Christian community, the goal in listening and discussion is to come near to people in real encounters. As they learn to know themselves, what they think and feel, and as they are allowed to express themselves, they can begin to question and to learn. If they speak from where they are instead of where we think they ought to be, they can grow. The Christian teacher dares to engage in such encounter because he too has been encountered by a forgiving God. He is now able to be a person for others, freed from his own ego needs. As God has come near us in the Incarnation, we are free in Christ to be present with one another.

Being present with each other

Discussion is, above all, a being present with each other, a being present which is intentional, full of energy, a traveling with the other where that person goes mentally and emotionally. We let loose of our own journey that we

75

might fully see what the other sees, hear the sounds the other describes, feel the other's pain, as the person uses words, inadequate as they might be, to convey it.

Listening requires the energy of alertness. A yawn may be all that is necessary to discourage a person from telling us any more. A glance at the wall clock says, "You've talked long enough now." More blatantly, we often listen only far enough to spark an idea in our own mind, at which time we jump in and take off in the direction we want to go, or mentally stop hearing in order to keep track of our own thought until we have time to speak.

The person to whom we are listening may be hesitant, repetitious, or witty but evasive. Waiting with someone while she learns to articulate and learns through that articulation takes patience. Most people think four times faster than they can listen. It is hard work to listen. We quietly rejoice when a person has succeeded in putting into words what she has been seeing and feeling, when she can speak her beliefs. Now they are really hers! The listening of discussion is a bit like midwifery. We wait with, bear with, but only the woman can give birth.

Many of us err in listening not quite far enough. For years I would listen intently, catch the ideas of others and then finish their sentences for them. They would seem delighted, "Yes, you know what I mean," but that experience would have been more valuable for them had I waited patiently until they discovered the words for themselves.

Learning to listen may be a major task for the talkative. Turning down the sound of one's own mental adventures to tune into another is difficult. One might assume that a quiet person would find listening easier. That may be, but not necessarily so. A silent person may not be present at all, or may never have wrestled with ideas enough to understand another easily. The person who values the learning potential in discussion may find the teaching skill of listening one of the most difficult to learn.

The role of the leader

At the end of a term, students in evaluating a class may say, "The best times were when we got off the subject and just talked." My response is, "I'm glad you enjoyed that, but you were never off the subject." Setting the learning environment is important so that discussion can touch people's lives. The perimeters of that learning environment are as broad as those lives.

A discussion class is not merely a "bull session." People who have scheduled time to come together want content and direction. The leader takes responsibility for setting the perimeters of the discussion. Leadership should be determined, accepted, and exercised. Sharing leadership is appropriate, but an absence of leadership is uncomfortable for all.

What is the role of teacher/leader in discussion? The leader will be occupied with listening and with constant decision-making. The leader needs to assess where the group is going, keep content relevant to the entire group, enable others to feel able to contribute an idea, provide bridges from one person to another, especially when they see the situation from an alternative developmental perspective. Direction is important for discussion, but allowing people to speak and then withdrawing that freedom by correcting, manipulating, or controlling too tightly is more frustrating for a group than never having had a chance to discuss at all.

If discussion is a primary style of learning for a class, students will begin to come with questions and situations from life that have arisen during the week. The wise

77

leader and the caring group will give time for each to identify the topics each may have for the session. From time to time the group will need to discuss its own skills in discussion. Most groups, with care and patience, can grow in their skills of listening to others, thereby learning how to learn from each other.

Staying in the leadership role when, to an observer, no leadership is being exercised, is quiet work. One does not have to coach a baseball team by being the pitcher, but neither does the coach withdraw to the stands or mentally go home.

Can the leader, at any given point, gently guide the group forward? Or have the members roamed away aimlessly? Or has another taken leadership by talking the most or the most impressively, one who may not have in mind the welfare of the entire group?

In watching a seminarian lead a discussion group in a responsible, enabling way, I often notice when, having stimulated a vigorous discussion, the leader is no longer able to lead.

"When did you no longer feel able to guide the group?" I ask.

The response may be, "When Joe and Marie seemed to take over with their debate; I knew the rest of the group was bored, but I didn't know what to do."

Learning what to do at such a point is learning to teach through discussion. The group is more comfortable to share freely when they know the teacher is quietly, but intently, continuing to care for the learning environment of the entire group.

Silence: an important part of discussion

Silence is a part of discussion. A group will need time to think, to reflect, to digest, and to gather new thoughts.

Active silences are healthy. Particularly among adult groups, the anticipatory hush may signal a readiness for the leader to move on after one subject has run its course. An inactive silence signals the group is no longer present and needs more content or stimulus. The nervous silence signals something is not right in the group's relationships, and perhaps they need to talk about that.

Discussion methods raise questions about the goals of group participation. Need everyone speak? Should everyone at least be able to speak? Discovering signals of eye contact and body motion, being aware of what is going on nonverbally, is essential. The leader may want to check occasionally to see if he or she is reading signals of involvement accurately. The experienced discussion group will eventually take responsibility for quieting those who might dominate and encouraging those who are more hesitant to share.

At times one person, perhaps because he needs attention or has been invited to share in a group so rarely, begins to talk as never before. Others in the group will listen, for a while. They may become uneasy, fearful of the person's later regretting all that he has said. Or they may become bored and restless, dissatisfied that their own needs are not being met. The leader may need to bring the individual to a stopping point, giving affirmation for what was shared and indicating a willingness to talk more with the person later. It is important to check back after class to see where the individual is at this point and if and when you might follow up on what the person has begun to work on.

At times the leader might become so hooked into what is being said that he or she loses objectivity. When this happens, the leader can no longer be aware of all group members, no longer be about the task of enabling learning. But the leader can be a genuine group member, sharing honestly and openly his or her own opinions. Doing this, while maintaining the relationship of leader responsibility, is a challenge.

When is discussion appropriate?

Beyond the value to the individual learner of growth through her own verbalization, is discussion an effective method for learning content? No matter how thoroughly prepared a teacher is, no matter how finely researched the presentation, no one leader will know everything about any given subject. Open discussion invites a collecting of wisdom that is comprehensive, rich, and balanced.

Discussion works well for the teacher if the subject is one on which the teacher is well informed and with which the teacher is comfortable. The teacher is free to allow the discussion to emerge, and no matter which way the group goes, he or she will be able to guide, redirect, clarify, and summarize at various points.

A subject about which all class members have some familiarity aids discussion. Teacher and students alike may bring much to a discussion topic such as "the Christian family." When the subject is "New Developments in School Vouchers for Religious Instruction," the teacher may choose discussion, but do added research, so that discussion is not merely a sharing of opinions and misinformation. When the subject is relatively unfamiliar to most group members, the teacher may well decide on a lecture style, at least to begin the session.

Discussion is an appropriate primary learning style when the group members have within their own experience and educational backgrounds observations and insights which can be shared and on which the group can build. Even though the flow of ideas in a discussion may not produce as neat an outline as a lecture, the comprehensive nature of the content covered is often remarkable. A recalling and summarizing of the session often surprises the group as to how much they have said and how much they remember and will remember, because they have given birth to the ideas themselves.

Crafts and conversation

Discussion is not recess from learning, but can be the heart and substance of learning. Likewise the traditional "craft" period in the church school has been thought of as a release from heavy indoctrination. During the late 1950s and 1960s many Sunday schools threw out traditional lesson books. Through creative projects the children were to have a happy experience in Sunday school. To think that crafts are Christian education is to shortchange the students. After almost a generation of making collages, is it any wonder that our children do not know the riches of the Scriptures or the doctrine of their church, and turn hungrily to the cults?

How can the craft period become a place where substantive Christian education takes place? First, the teacher needs to be a person who is well grounded and growing in Scripture, in the teachings of the church, one who can verbalize that faith in ordinary language. Secondly, the teacher will be one who enjoys using the crafts time (or any other informal activity time) as an occasion to be engaged with the students in meaningful conversation.

As one listens to a group of people working together pulling dandelions in the churchyard, preparing a meal in the kitchen, or putting away Christmas decorations, what do they talk about? What are the concerns on their hearts and minds? Is it politics? Is it a recent television program? Is it a difficult situation at school? Is it illness in the home? How are they reacting? What developmental stage is operative?

As the teacher moves about the room, affirming the creative work the students are doing, helping with a difficult part, providing more glue or locating the scissors, there will be opportunity to listen, to converse with the students about their lives and about God's activity in the world in the midst of life. There will be opportunities for making connection, for inductive thinking, for students to come to their own conclusions, all while they are talking and working.

Ways to sabotage discussion

Often a potentially good discussion is sabotaged by the leader herself. Discussion is not: (1) giving a second lecture; (2) asking "guess-what-I'm-thinking" questions; (3) competitive listening.

A second lecture

Excited about the material, the teacher asks a question. A group member responds, adding a new thought. Instead of replying, "Yes, that's interesting. Could you say more about that?" the leader remembers some other material not covered and launches into a second lecture, overwhelming the tentative student with thoughts not yet fully formed.

Or the teacher, needing to defend the subject presented will listen to the student's response and then proceed to correct the student, adding more facts. The teacher may merely repeat information the student gave, in different words, therefore keeping hold of the position as information giver.

Many presentations will have time for "discussion following." Usually this means the speaker entertains questions from the group. These questions may be legitimate things about which the student is wondering; or, having learned the role well, the student may work at forming questions which will please the speaker. The teacher receives such responses as signs of recognition and approval, often affirming the student with, "That's a good question." (Isn't every question good if it is a genuine offering of the student?)

At a continuing-education event for pastors an afternoon speaker presented a subject of great interest. The moderator announced that at 7 P.M. the speaker would be available for those who wanted to engage in dialog with the speaker. About 30 people returned at 7 P.M. At about 7:45 the speaker, who had a plane to catch, was whisked away by the moderator. People sat, silenced for a second, and then began to disperse. With the answering-person gone, the discussion was over.

Four of us, still strangers to each other, looked at the empty speaker's stand and then at each other. Almost in unison, we turned our chairs toward one another and decided we could go on discussing without the speaker. We had given ourselves permission to talk, and to learn from each other. Quickly introducing ourselves, we continued the discussion for two hours.

Discussion group members should at all times have permission to be learners, talking not to please the teacher or not to be "straight men" for the lecturer to entertain some more. Particularly for adults, who have been schooled in dependent learning, moving from being audience to being interdependent, active listeners and speakers is a difficult, but exciting, transition. A teacher might ask, "If I had to catch a plane, or if I left the room, could the discussion go on without me?"

Guess-what-I'm-thinking questions

A teacher sometimes uses discussion to go where he wants to go. The students become mechanical answer-people in a fill-in-the-blank lecture style: "The causes of our crisis in ethics are many. What's one of them?" Or "Who is it that stays with you in all kinds of trouble?"

"Jesus," someone answers. (When in doubt, the students learn to answer, "Jesus"!)

Pastors giving children's sermons often make the mistake of asking children to fill in the blanks of their thoughts. The children's sermon begins:

> "This morning I have here with me a box of crackers. They remind me of a Bible story. Does anybody know which one?"

> The children, more interested in eating the crackers than in talking about them, and certainly not at a developmental level where analogy and metaphor is their primary mode of thinking, have no idea which Bible story the pastor is thinking about. Not really caring, but bid to perform, they bravely take some guesses, "Jesus feeds the 5000," or "The children of Israel in the wilderness."

How much more honest for the pastor to welcome the children to the front of the church, to make a straightforward presentation, and then to converse with the children, to go with them where they go. This is risky, particularly in front of all those adults in the congregation. Our contrived "discussions" may show we are working too hard at making things turn out right. If we are going

84

to have children's sermons (and there is indeed value in adults "overhearing" the gospel while not directly engaged), then we had either better make straight presentation, or be willing to dialog honestly with the children. In doing the latter we might be surprised by joy with the marvelous ways children do express the gospel, conversationally: "God really does take care of us. Now can I share a cracker with my uncle out there?"

The greatest learning is that which comes in response to our own questions. Curiosity must precede discovery. Questioning is a key to learning, if the questioning is done by the learner!

Open-ended questions are helpful. Questions which affirm and encourage more thought are important.[1] Far too often teachers use questions to probe in hurtful, inappropriate ways. Questions which entrap or questions that divide the "smart from the dumb" force a particular behavior but do not foster real learning.

Some questioners ask but give no regard for serious answers. Others ask so that the respondent will be either a winner or a loser. A discussion leader may find that in removing "grading talk" from his or her language, the discussion flows much better. "That's good." "That's not quite right." These often-heard comments are unnecessary crutches that foster dependent learning.

The rhetorical question, particularly when employed to show the number of unanswered problems which lie before us, is a challenge to growth and action: Questions that arouse curiosity, questions that invite new adventures in thought, questions that are open-ended and affirming encourage discussion. Exciting is the class where the teacher asks questions not to merely follow her own train of thought but to know what the students are thinking, and in the process becomes curious with them.

Competitive listening

Learning together may lead everyone in the group, including the teacher, into a place they have never been before. It is the very opposite of getting things under control. It is cooperative, not competitive. It is exciting, not tame.

Many people, however, listen precisely to win, as Lew Holm, friend and former colleague, writes in this essay:

> If listening had been a competitive sport, I could have been a superstar. I'd probably have played in the world series and won the car.
>
> I listened to win. No matter what anyone said to me, I topped it.
>
> Have you had a run of bad luck? Mine was twice as bad and lasted longer.
>
> Somewhere along the line I learned to separate the idea of competition for the idea of listening. It happened when a good friend of mine confronted me with the question of why I felt I had to win our conversasions. I'm deeply grateful to him for such honest friendship.
>
> Listening is a lot more fun for me now. Sometimes I listen for content and learn useful things. At other times, as when I listen in on a discussion of politics, I listen analytically or critically, weighing the arguments against what I already know. Occasionally I have even been known to listen creatively, putting the speaker's wisdom together with mine and coming up with an inspiring idea, even beyond what the speaker had said.
>
> I'd never have been able to enjoy listening if it hadn't been for my friend. I would still have been playing the listening contest and losing my friends one after the other.

Henri Nouwen speaks of learning which needs things controlled or competitive as *violent*. Such discussion is merely an intellectual battle from which people tend to return more close-minded than when they entered, more like soldiers reloading their rifles than friends shaking hands. Teaching can be a redemptive process if it is evocative. As Henri Nouwen says, "Each tries to evoke in the other his respective potentials and make them available to each other." [2]

Listening that is competitive or controlling for my own sake (because I need to prove myself, or protect myself) is not good teaching. On the other hand, discussion that is merely passive and comfortable avoids the confrontative edge which spurs us on to change and to make a difference in the world.

By their fruits you will know them

When the Christian learning community takes God seriously and in Christ is free to take each other seriously, listening may be a pathway to action. Discussion provides opportunities for the Spirit to work through a group in ways no individual would have thought about. One ninth-grade class discovered that "You shall not kill" and "You shall not steal" meant helping and befriending as well. Having discovered this idea, they challenged each other to the global meaning and set about on their own finding out about world hunger and planning a fast to raise money for hungry people.

But learning set loose did not stop there. In discussions at the weekend fast retreat they discovered, "We really don't need to eat as much as we do. And we really don't need to have refreshments at every church meeting."

Their discussion spun off take-home, long-range plans for a change in life-style.

One sees the results of open-ended discussion in which people come to grips with life as it is. A woman in a Lenten class began to discover for the first time the meaning of the Psalms. She asked about alienation. The class listened as she talked about her pain because of her own unwillingness to forgive. The next week she came back and quietly said she had prayed about her daughter—and then had picked up the telephone and called her.

An ecumenical discussion group learned to listen beyond old fears and competitions. The members from one church helped repair a basement wall in the host church. "We've noticed that crack every night we've been sitting here," someone said. One wall was repaired; many other walls were broken down.

Such fruits of the Spirit indeed come. But although our redemption in Christ is complete, our freedom to live out the Christ life, to listen *for* as well as *to* the other, is a new gift each day. The controlling, competitive self, still bound by a need to prove or protect the self, struggles within us. We do not want to listen to or learn from another. In fact, we are not merely passive in this regard but carry on an active resistance, placing roadblocks in front of one another.

Effectiveness training

Thomas Gordon's TET, Teacher Effectiveness Training, and PET, Parent Effectiveness Training, with many spin-off programs identifies 12 roadblocks to effective listening. While Gordon does not deal with the ongoing human problem which we call sin, our continuously wanting to manipulate each other, we can adapt some of Gordon's work. Building on the nondirective counseling work of Carl Rogers, effectiveness training is precise and concrete and has helped many people improve listening skills and understand their own feelings. It leaves room for children to own their own feelings and come to the solution of their own problems. Gordon believes that communication skills that facilitate problem solving can be learned. The language of acceptance is powerful. Referring to problem-solving, not to general conversation, Gordon advocates four skills: [3]

1. *Passive listening* (silence).   This gives a student the opportunity to talk. Being quiet long enough to listen is a good beginning.

2. *Acknowledgment responses.*   Verbal and nonverbal signs indicate that the teacher is "going with" the student. Some are nodding, leaning forward, indicating, "I see." They show a student you are still attentive.

3. *Door openers.*   Although overuse can make these meaningless, when used honestly they facilitate student thinking. "Would you like to say more about that?" or "It sounds as if you have strong feelings about that."

4. *Active listening.*   Continued, nonjudgmental interaction. The student may ask, "How long is it till class is over?" The student may merely want to know the time. Or he may be anxious about any number of things which are going to happen later that day. Or he may be uncomfortable in the classroom situation, not understanding what is going on, or angry with another child. The teacher's response, "You are concerned about when class will be over," enables the student to go on and say more.

Learning from inside out

God's creation of human potential is awe-inspiring. Teaching to correct, or to change a person's ideas or behavior is to miss discovering who the person really is at this particular stage of development. It denies the student's ability to learn inductively. The class that learns to listen to one another will not only have the joy of personal learning breakthroughs, but may enrich the content of the discussion.

But listening and discussion is not the whole of education. Our own human development must be intersected with the cross at each life stage; we need the Word from outside ourselves. Discussion is a vital learning style, but only one facet of educational ministry.

Chapter 4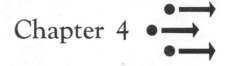

Inductive Study

"Sally, you read with me." He puts his finger by the next word, and Sally reads, "Come." The teacher goes on, "Come into his presence with singing." Sally is elated because she and the teacher are reading the Scriptures together.

Many would define Christian education as the acquisition of facts, the understanding of concepts concerning the Christian faith. They would see any method which does not promote the development of knowledge and skills as nontraditional.

If we speak about tradition, however, we would need to go back far enough, before the memory books our parents had, and we would see Jesus using life experience rather than filling in blanks in workbooks. Of course, in teaching Jewish people, he assumed a certain knowledge of the law which the people had indeed "learned."

For centuries children learned about the faith from watching their parents and other adults live the faith, rather than through attending classes. For thousands of years people have handed down the tradition through storytelling. The "traditional" way to teach Sunday school (the Sunday school itself only being 200 years old) is certainly broader than having children look up a Bible verse and write down what it says.

Acquiring facts and knowledge and writing down answers is only one facet of educational ministry. However, there is indeed an important place for acquiring knowledge and being tested on such learning. Understanding and skill building are crucial components of education. This is only one facet of learning, but it is a meat-and-potatoes style. Because it is central to classroom work, we should understand this style in order to use it effectively.

People want to be learners

Children and adults alike want to be challenged to work, to know more than they knew last week. They want to be learners. Most significantly, people need to learn how to be learners.

What is a young person learning when she is engaged in pronouncing the books of the Bible? The child may be thinking, *I can say these words. They tickle my tongue. They are long and sound important. I can say them just like my teacher says them.* Or the child may think, *This is hard. I can't do it. There are too many parts to that word. I can't do it and teacher is mad at me.*

In the first instance the child, who has already heard the words many times, now tries out a new skill of saying them and delights in a new skill. She is moving along the path to capable adulthood and sees the teacher, whom she admires, at that place which is the child's goal. In the second instance, the child learns she is incapable. The child has not proceeded step by step in skill building and cannot make the jump. She becomes afraid of disapproval and may make a subconscious decision not to try again, or at least not to try out loud.

People are created to learn. They learn best when led from where they are to where they need to go. As they are led into a new area, as they are taught inductively, there is a direct relationship between attitude and new ability.

In inductive learning the students' own knowledge and skills are called forth in such a way that they can move on by themselves from the place they were to the next stage of learning. The various abilities and pieces of information now come together so that at this new stage they can use them to summarize and generalize. The students then have a solid foundation from which they can move on to acquire more knowledge and skills.

The learning edge

If a person is working precisely at the learning edge of his ability, the individual will be challenged and able. If the person is working at any other place than the learning edge, he will either be bored or frustrated. This is particularly noticeable with adult learners. They will tell with their absence from class the next time that they were insulted and did not want to waste their time "learning" something they already knew. Or they will say with their absence that they were embarrassed and could not bear coming again to a class where they did not understand what was going on.

Children usually cannot use their absence to show their boredom and frustration—after all, "it is a child's business to be in school." And, to a certain extent, show less boredom because they thrive on repetition. When *Sesame Street* began over a dozen years ago, adults were amazed that so many segments would be repeated, even within the same program. Children delighted in seeing favorite segments again and again, a fact the producers had learned from observing young viewers watch advertisements. The child is pleased to see the familiar, to test out his developing knowledge and skill: "Yes, I *do* know the number seven!"

But there is a limit to repetition in skill reinforcement. Children who have no choice about returning to the next class session will reveal by their *mis*behavior: "I am bored. I want to be challenged."

In *How Children Fail* John Holt writes about children being afraid or bored. Fear and failure go hand in hand. He says that we destroy children's capacity to learn by making them afraid—afraid to ask, afraid to be curious. Or, "We encourage children to act stupidly, not only by scaring and confusing them, but by boring them. . . . We tell ourselves that this drudgery, this endless busywork, is good preparation for life, and we fear that without it children would be hard to 'control.' " [1]

All who are engaged in educational ministry will agree that we should not make children, youth, or adults afraid of failure or bored. We want them to find their learning edge. Even if we as teachers pledge ourselves to meet each student at his learning edge, what about the child's part? Is the child not responsible in some way for his own learning? What about motivation? Is it up to the teacher to find the precise hole in the socket, and then plug in learning? And even if the teacher does, will the energy flow? Will the person be led into new learning?

Holt is correct in diagnosing the ways we contribute to

children's failure to learn: "We adults destroy most of the intellectual and creative capacity of children by the things we do to them or make them do." [2]

However, rather than being encouraged to find ways to teach which produce capable learners, many educators, in the public sphere as well as in the Christian community, have become depressed and defeated at their own propensity to harm children's learning growth. But our ultimate goal is not to realize how *teachers* fail; our goal is to realize the difficulty of the teaching task because of the human problems of teachers *and* learners, and to find strength in Christ to begin anew in spite of those difficulties.

Created to learn

Motivation in learning is a complex topic—a theological, as well as an educational, question. The infant and adult display a curious spirit. But our broken human condition also means that, to some extent, we avoid healthy growth. We manage to fail without any help from teachers. Others also provide barriers, unintentionally and intentionally, as a means to "control," and so the problem is complicated.

Proceeding along the growth continuum, learning how to learn, is no longer natural to us. We are created curious, with energy and potential for growth, but individually and collectively, we confound that process. To live in grace in the Christian teaching/learning community is to know the depth and complexity of the problems of learning and to be set free in new Spirit-filled relationships to learn and grow as we were created to do.

This attitude is essential if we are to break out of our need to compel people to meet our standards of achievement or to control people by keeping classes safely dull. Learning is a gift of new relationships and new potential.

Designed to develop

We are created to learn; we are designed to develop. We are rarely aware of a child's physical growth, day-by-day, even when a teenager grows four inches in one summer. And yet there are those transitions from one developmental stage to another which cause us to marvel. During one week I was aware that each of our three children was changing in significant ways: the baby was learning to see, the toddler was learning to talk, and our first grader was learning to read. The sheer joy of achieving each one of those precious skills! Life is intended to be filled with "I cans"—I can see, I can talk, I can remember, I can compare, I can analyze, I can evaluate, I can synthesize.

Erik Erikson believes that we move from one developmental stage to the next by passing through a crisis or transition. One cannot say the exact age at which a person will move from one stage to another, although there are age ranges. But a person does not move from stage one to stage four without passing through two and three. We cannot teach as though a person were at one level, when in fact the person is not.

Erikson's psychosocial stages	Approximate age
Basic trust vs. mistrust	0-2 years
Autonomy vs. shame/doubt	2-3½ years
Initiative vs. guilt	3½-6 years
Industry vs. inferiority	6-12 years
Identity vs. role diffusion	13-21 years
Intimacy vs. isolation	the 20s
Generativity vs. self-absorption	late 20s to 50s
Integrity vs. despair	50s and beyond

Jean Piaget has done extensive work on cognitive development, and his work is the basis for understanding the developing self and intellectual capacities for reasoning at various ages.

LEVEL 1. *Sensorimotor period:* The child's world is a collection of the objects and actions which are immediately present, with the child at the center. *Approximate ages:* 0-1½ years.

LEVEL 2. *Preoperational thought period:* Things are what they appear to be. The child can use words, mental pictures to think, but is unconcerned about logic. *Approximate ages:* 2-6 years.

LEVEL 3. *Concrete operational thought period:* The child is learning to organize and order logical relationships but cannot hypothesize or think abstractly. *Approximate ages:* 7-12 years.

LEVEL 4. *Formal operations period:* The person is thinking abstractly, developing logical thinking based on propositional statements. He can think about thinking.[3] *Approximate ages:* 13 and beyond.

Four inductive-learning skills

As teachers in the Christian learning community we are committed to helping individuals develop to their full created potential. We are cognizant of developmental stages and want to teach at the growing edge. In broad strokes, let us look at four areas of inductive learning: 1) *to question,* 2) *to know,* 3) *to speak,* and 4) *to be able.* These are basic to the very process of learning inductively.

1. To question

To be curious, to hunger to know is an important basis for inductive learning. The learner must learn to question. In Chapter 3 we discussed the inappropriateness of "guess-what-I'm-thinking" questions. There is a world of difference between "asking with" and "asking at." To question with people, to encourage questions, to foster a questioning spirit helps a person become a learner and move from one development stage to the next.

Luther's Small Catechism used the question-answer technique.

> Luther, of course, had the task of producing the answers to the question, "What does this mean?" The burden was on him as a teacher to come up with the answers in such a style that children on hearing them, would be helped to understand. By our day, however, the catechization tradition within Lutheranism has reversed the roles. Until recently, it was common for the teacher to ask a question and the students had the responsibility to give the answer. Not only that, but often students had to give just exactly the "correct" answer and nothing else. It is easy to see why children felt more obligated to give the correctly *worded* answer than to seek understanding about what was being asked.[4]

To teach in such a way that students are encouraged to raise their own questions is to facilitate inductive learning. Questioning is not a form of ignorance, but a sign that a person has begun to learn. The infant begins to search, physically interacting with the world around, gradually discovering that the world is separate from himself. During the preoperational period, the very young child begins to question with words, asserting his own autonomy, and eventually initiating his own pursuits.

The grade-school child is able to use logic to form his questions, but questioning which uses abstract thought must usually wait for the adolescent years.

"What does this mean?" and "What does this mean for us?" are crucial questions which the growing Christian will ask when excited about the content of material.

A teacher might raise questions that puzzle the child in order to stimulate more questions, "Why are there so many German names in our telephone book and so many Scandinavian names in the book of the town ten miles down the road? Why did the Irish immigrants come in one decade and not another? When did the Puerto Ricans begin to come to New York? Why did the refugee family from Laos move to California after just a year here in Iowa? Where will I be living 10 years from now?"

One cannot ask questions about which one knows little. "I don't even know enough to ask," many an adult will say as the reason for being quiet in Sunday morning class. The child who tastes church history at age seven and again at age 10 and again at age 15 will have learned something so he or she can begin to be curious. The child will have hooks on which to hang new learnings. In his church history for children Roland Bainton says:

> If when the world becomes Christian, churchmen become lordly as senators, and emperors banish bishops, what should the serious Christian do? "Get out of the world," answered some. "Go to the desert. Flee the world, flee the cities. Go back to the fields where the farmer sings psalms at the plow. Flee the murderous emperors and sleek ministers. Flee everybody and live all alone." The people who did this were called hermits and monks. "Hermit" means one who lives in the desert. "Monk" means one who lives alone. The first monks were hermits. But later "hermit" was used of one who lived entirely alone, and "monk" of one who

> left the world of cities and families to live apart with a group of other monks. The movement began in Egypt.[5]

The young Christian has some sense of the church of the fourth century. Somewhere later the child will make the connection that Martin Luther was a monk. What was Luther's struggle? The child learned from Bainton's history that the Christian church has an important history on the continent of Africa. With growing maturity, the questions take on deeper and broader perspective. Where is the church today? Why do we behave as if to be a Christian is to be a European? What is our mission stance in the worldwide church today? What is it to be a Christian in a pluralistic society? Is there any value in the move to the desert? How can I be a Christian in a pseudo-Christian society? Do I retreat from the world?

And so the questioning Christian mind grows to adulthood—having heard about the history of the faith, having learned how to question in order to learn, in order to question some more.

2. To know

An essential component of inductive learning is knowledge. In this book I give a great deal of attention to the attitude of teacher and learner, to feelings, to creating the learning environment, to experiencing. All of these, without knowledge, without facts, without information, would have little substance. Learning cannot, however, be measured by the information given by the teacher. Learning takes place only when knowledge becomes the possession of the student. When knowledge is truly owned the person is able to use it to grow inductively. Taking account of information that is handed out in a class is

100

quite simple. Measuring what each student actually knows is much more difficult.

When does a child know, "I am adopted"? The adoptive parent does not keep the fact a secret, but tells the child in words from early on. The words take on meaning gradually. The child has "always known" and yet continues to grow in understanding of what adoption means in her life.

When does a child learn "Lamb of God, pure and holy"? The child hears it sung in the worshiping community. She soon sings the words herself. One child of six was even able to articulate how he learned words and music. "I listen to what the grown-up next to me sings, and I sing it right after, real quick, so it sounds like I'm singing at the same time." Soon he knew these hymns, music and words, and could sing them anytime, anywhere, whether or not a grown-up was next to him singing them first.

Indeed if all knowledge could be learned through singing, for many of us learning would be much easier. We rarely forget the words to a song once loved and learned. As we visit in hospitals and nursing homes and sing those old hymns with the dying, we know that although eyesight is gone and ability to reason is fading, nothing can take away what was learned so many years ago. What was first learned has been filled full with a lifetime of meaning. Using Piaget's concepts, the child may learn the words at the preoperational level, conceiving of images in concrete ways. As she grows more mature, the child fills those original concepts full of abstract and relational meanings.

We actually have stored up in our minds much more than we realize, a filing cabinet of information, much dusty and unused. That knowledge we actively use soon after we have acquired it has the most potential for serving us well. We use that knowledge as a foundation on which to inquire and build more complex knowledge.

But we also know things that we don't know we know. Recently my sister brought to my house our old family mantle clock. Since our mother's death two years before, my sister had had the clock in her home, but the chiming tended to keep her awake.

I was delighted to have the clock. Noting that there was worn tape sealing the back of the clock, I decided to replace the tape to keep out household dust.

I wound the clock. But now a problem occurred to me. How could I manually start the pendulum with the back sealed? Without an instant of thought on how to solve the problem, I instinctively tilted the right front corner slightly. The clock began to tick. "Instinctively" is not the correct word, for I had *learned* to start the clock that way. Not that I had ever done it before, but I had watched my mother years before start the mantle clock in precisely that manner. I had learned how to start the mantle clock, even though I had never done it and had not seen her start it that way in over 25 years. Knowing is a complex process —beyond our "knowing" about it. But we can provide a rich variety of ways in which the student can grow in knowledge at his level.

The love of knowing can be facilitated by the Christian community. From early on the child should know that the Bible and Christian books are a rich source of knowledge. The church library, often merely a refuge for discarded books from member's homes, needs loving, knowledgeable attention from someone who loves books *and* people.

Church librarians and resource centers need to be inviting, accessible, and useable. One church set up a reading corner in the large church narthex. Small tables and chairs made the young Christians feel welcome as they came to church, as the grown-ups around them talked.

A reading program or a reading group for adults is essential not only for the adults themselves, but for the children who will grow up thinking it is normal for Christians to read and research on their own through the resources of their own church.

Children like to own books. Congregations that give good Christian literature, church history, and resource books are making a helpful investment which lasts much beyond candy and favors. I have yet to see an elementary child not delighted to receive a dictionary of his own, or a junior-high youngster to receive a thesaurus or a Bible history.

In learning "to know," tests have their place. But they have often been misused. They seem an antithesis of grace. Indeed, although Luther's Catechisms were written that laity might learn the riches of Christian knowledge, it was not long before "the catechism became a weapon in the hands of the church and state authorities to enforce loyalty to Lutheranism and obedience to the regulations of the Lutheran state clergy . . . not being able to recite it was sufficient reason in some areas and towns for keeping people away from Holy Communion." [6]

Many adults will recall their own examination before confirmation and remember the fear and shame associated with such public testing. Overreaction, however, may produce an era in which educators believe Christian education should never be rigorous. The excitement of growing in knowledge need not be coupled with fear of embarrassment or failure. Recall Erikson's autonomy vs. shame/doubt, initiative vs. guilt, and industry vs. inferiority stages. Although they are loosely associated with chronological ages, each new stage requires reworking past solutions. At each stage of life the growing person needs to be free of shame, doubt, guilt, and inferiority in order to be autonomous, taking initiative for his or her own growth in knowledge.

Inductive learning needs the companion of teacher assessment. The teacher needs to know what the students are grasping from information being communicated. Where is the teaching leading them in their own thinking? Which concepts came across? What went right past the class? What misinformation did they learn? Testing may test a teacher more than students.

Testing need not pit student against student. The student who is tested against himself or herself with reinforcement of correct answers and correction of errors will be encouraged to continue to try. Computers can provide this kind of immediate feedback which challenges, but does not malign, the student's personhood.

Cooperative small-group testing provides a noncompetitive joint research project. There is an air of excitement and deliberation, an urgency to share their findings. Group exams can provide for review, reinforcement, clarification, and summarization. Contrastingly, observe a class taking an exam in which the test is geared so that a certain percentage pass and a certain percentage fail. One sees heads down. Students may feel fear, pressure, and power. The corporate nature of learning is gone. Mutuality is replaced by opposition. Individual ranking looms to the forefront: "How will I measure up in relation to others?"

I have conversed with some teachers who actually enjoy wielding such power. The fate of the students is in their hands. One young man said, "It's a way I can finally be in control after all those years of my teachers having all the answers in their hands."

Testing can be fun. One objective for a good test is that students come out of the test knowing more than they did when they started. The teacher should ask, "What activities and questions can I use that will help students put things together in new ways so they can summarize and synthesize as well as recall?" Such testing does not limit learning (as it does when the only possibilities are being right or wrong). The challenge of preparing questions which break open the learning to new levels may be shared with students themselves contributing to the test with one or more questions they have prepared from their own review.

And what about grading? Society lives by the principle that being number 1 is best. In the Christian community we confess that we are gifted by God with individual abilities. How can I the teacher evaluate work without communicating worthlessness to a student? One way is by giving personal evaluation rather than comparative evaluation. One-on-one conferences give the student and teacher opportunity to pinpoint specific strengths and needs. A written evaluation to the family of a confirmand involves parents in student learning. Home visits—not just for misbehavior, but as a regular way of conversing about growth in knowledge and skills—combine evaluation with affirmation of the importance of the individual.

3. To speak

The third broad area for our consideration is to be able to speak, to communicate. A person is led into learning through being able to put into words the understandings already possessed. The Christian classroom becomes a laboratory, a place to try out ideas, to put them into new formulations of words. The Christian classroom becomes the gymnasium in which to exercise and to be prepared to speak the faith in the world. In early childhood youngsters speak the words they have heard and delight in the ability to use that knowledge immediately. Why do we accept as natural for adults a wide separation of these two skills?

There is a ministry of words, but it is not applying a slick coat of easy words which covers people's problems, and smothers the people. Knowledge of the faith is learned when one can translate it into the language of the people with whom one lives. As Christian children or adults find meaning in the gospel and speak it meaningfully to those with whom they live the creeds take on even deeper meaning. The child whose world was egocentric, now turns outward. The developing Christian adult has weighed and compared the faith with other ideologies and now can speak with conviction in the world of ideas.

The Christian classroom is a place to challenge one another. A classroom of teachers, meeting regularly, is a place to challenge their own communication of the faith. "How do you put the doctrine of justification by grace alone into words an eight-year-old can understand?" "How should you put that into words for an adult who has low self-esteem?"

To grow in ability to communicate means to listen, to watch, and to love. Recently I spent two days at a state hospital-school for the mentally retarded. I had visited that same institution 20 years before. I knew I would see vast changes, because of the progress society has made in awareness, attitude and insight regarding the retarded. Whereas 20 years ago, many were bedfast with little expectation of growth and development, residents were now out of bed, up and busy. Wheelchairs were designed so that whatever the physical disabilities, the person could be upright and have eye contact with other people.

One high school volunteer I was observing met a non-verbal resident coming for prevocational classes. The resident, Jeannie, came bounding into the room, delighted to be there, making unintelligible sounds. The high school student, obviously glad to see Jeannie, greeted her with the same sounds, put her arms around the resident, and hugged her.

Later I told the high school volunteer that she was speaking the gospel in the language to the people. She was meeting the resident where she was. They were communicating with eyes, sounds, hearts, and total being. And Jeannie was also learning to speak the gospel. Although nonverbal, she had received the love of God communicated with continuity and commitment and she was vibrant. She was no longer sitting in a chair with eyes turned downward. She was learning to communicate with her eyes, her smile, and her friendly cooperation.

Many times Christians who do have ability to speak, live with eyes turned downwards. They may "know" much more than Jeannie ever will, but they have not learned how to communicate.

One needs to be led into speaking so that one can continue to learn how to learn. As people develop their own skills in communication, at whatever level, they continue on the growth continuum. As we wrestle with words, our ability to analyze also grows.

4. To be able

If Christian education is *for* mission, the results of learning will be ministry. If one learns to know Christ, the result of such learning will be willingness and ability to follow Christ. Such learning results in discipline and discipleship.

There is a cry in the land today for more discipline in

the home, in the school, and in society as a whole. Open-ended learning modes need not be an enemy of good discipline. Christians need to learn how to live in ways that give expression to Christ's new life in them. In a life-long learning project, the Christian student needs to be guided in disciplined ways in order to become a disciplined person. We continue to learn new behaviors and abilities so that our faith can be expressed.

Christian discipline is not for its own sake, however, but for discipleship. How does one learn skill in discipleship? One learns to minister by being a ministering person. Although there is a newer book by this same name, I prefer a book written 100 years ago, *Ministering Children*. It is a book of delightful, rather sophisticated stories of children engaged in caring for the poor.

> In all aid rendered to others, the calling into exercise the best feelings of the heart, in both the giver and the receiver, is the most important object to be kept in view. To this end it is necessary that the talent of money be not suffered to assume an undue supremacy in the service of benevolence; let children be trained, and taught, and led aright . . . and they will not be slow to learn that they possess a personal influence everywhere.[7]

The young people in a confirmation class were involved in studying the Catechism, in crafts, and in music. They also had the daily assignment of taking the food the congregation had brought to the altar the day before to the neighborhood food-distribution center, Christian Community Action. The youth simply did it. The discipline of carrying food to the poor is one way of learning the skill and the habit of doing just that.

Children learn compassion by caring for God's creation, for people, for pets, and for the earth. Children learn the skills of helping by giving aid. All of these are vital if Christianity is to continue to be a faith which is known by its deeds.

As children grow to teenage years, they gradually begin to develop leadership skills. Inductive learning also takes place on a continuum. Many a youth leader has been sadly disappointed because his ninth graders wanted to decide on their own activities, but their plans fell through at the last moment. A person doesn't change from dependent follower to Christian leader overnight. We need to attend to the growing stage of "to be able."

Many adults today know how to listen, how to sit quietly, how to give an offering of money, and maybe even to organize a meeting. But they seem bewildered when challenged to new vistas of Christian service. They seem unable to learn. This may seem strange, for the very same people are able to *do* many things in their daily life.

We have neglected the skill of servanthood in our Christian instruction. People do care and want to help. But educational ministry must include constant attention to helping people develop skill in being able to be the disciplined disciples, the ministering people they have been called to be.

Inductive biblical study

In the Lutheran rite of Holy Baptism, the minister reminds parents of their obligations to the baptized children: "You should . . . faithfully bring them to the services of God's house, and teach them the Lord's Prayer, the Creed, and the Ten Commandments. As they grow in years you should place in their hands the Holy Scriptures and provide for their instruction in the Christian faith." [8]

In Baptism God gives us new life in Christ. This grace

109

is complete when the child is, from our human perspective, at a very early developmental stage. God's grace creates faith, but that faithful response of the human child continues to grow and change as the human being progresses through the developmental stages. [9]

Of course infants cannot read or understand the Bible, but the child is fully a Christian and should have the opportunity of receiving the biblical heritage according to the appropriate intellectual stage. Luther tells us that Scripture is so shallow a child can wade in it and so deep a grown person can drown in it.

Some educators have felt they need to protect children from the Bible. Ronald Goldman says, "Young children should not be exposed, for obvious reasons, to the painful, horrific and often morbid details of the Crucifixion, although they cannot be protected from knowledge of these events." [10]

In his "Basis for Development in Religious Education," Goldman advocates that the Bible should be used sparingly, "The Bible is the major source book of Christianity for it is written by adults for adults and is plainly not a children's book. To help children become familiar with it too early is to invite boredom and confusion." [11]

Goldman's remarks have some truth. Many people have not taken into consideration the fact that a child at Piaget's Concrete Operational Thought Period, who cannot think abstractly, will take biblical allegory literally. Even the "Kingdom of God is like . . ." parables, so often the subject of children's sermons, may send the child believing God is a candle living in a bushel basket. Adults may find this amusing, but such use of the Bible with the children does violence to the children Christ has invited to come to him.

On the other hand, Goldman misleads many into be-

110

lieving that children are not ready for the Bible. A proliferation of readiness-for-religion books have come on the market in recent years, colorful books about nature and feelings, but not a word about God. Such writers would have us believe these books are nontheological. How can one get ready for religion? Is any language nontheological? Such neutral words as "tree" and "friend" have a theological dimension. For words, like people, are incurably religious.

Looking at a Bible storybook she has just purchased, a Sunday school teacher thought a page was missing. Where was the crucifixion? The story went directly from Palm Sunday to Easter morning. This teacher asked her pastor, "But what do I say when the children ask, 'Why does it say Jesus is alive again? How and when did he die?' "

To paint an unduly gory picture of the crucifixion, or any other Bible story, as I have seen some comic books do, is harmful. But to keep the Bible from children until they are "ready" is to do harm by omission. The Bible is God's Word, ready for children—and adults—to claim as their own and to learn their way into. Use of the Bible with children and adults is not merely teaching that the Bible is true. Some Christians are so busy *defending* the Bible that they never find time to study it. God's Word does not need our defense. It *is* true and true for us, a gift for us to study, at all ages, in appropriate ways.

Preschool children

A teacher of preschool children can teach "from" the Bible. The mere presence of a Bible in the classroom is a beginning. Holding it, saying that the story you are telling is written in this Bible makes an impression and sets an attitude that this book is important: "God made us and loves us very much. God is always with us, wherev-

111

er we are. God has been with his people all the time. We know that because people from long ago have told us. The story of God and God's people is in the Bible. One of these stories is about. . . ."

The use of the Bible with preschoolers need not be limited to story. I recall a most exciting time with four-year-olds relating to the Psalms. We started reading Gerard Pottebaum's Paraphrase of Psalm 150: "Praise the Lord, Praise God uptown and downtown, Praise him with the blast of trumpets. Praise the Lord with the sliding trombone. Praise the Lord with flute and piccolo. Praise him with high-stepping marches. Praise him with beating drums. Praise him with whistles and horns. Let everything having breath praise the Lord. Alleluia! Alleluia! Yeah, yeah. Hurrah!" [12] The children picked up the chant, delighting in the rhythm. We began making accompanying sounds with our mouths, our hands, our feet—and soon we were all joyfully responding to the goodness of God. When our chant finally subsided, we experienced a joyful fatigue, an appropriate result of worship.

Who understands the word "God"? But using it with children in the midst of human experience communicates the presence of that God. With very young children we say a verse, "Grace to you and peace from God," simultaneously reaching out and becoming the hospitable human beings that God enables teachers to be. Even very small children learn to know the meaning of the words. The children are developing the trust and autonomy of which Erikson speaks. They are *knowing,* in Piaget's terms, knowing from the consistency of the actions and objects around them.

We open the Bible and say, "Sing aloud to God, our strength," and we say it again, week after week. We close

112

our eyes and pray and children begin to know what these words mean.

Beginning readers

The children are beginning to sight-read words. Their teacher has the Bible in the midst of them and reads, " 'Make a joyful noise to the Lord, all the lands. Serve the Lord with gladness!' Sally, you read with me." The teacher put his finger by the next word, and Sally reads, "Come." The teacher goes on, "Come into his presence with singing." Sally is elated because she and the teacher are reading the Scriptures together. The Scripture is becoming Sally's own. Her God-given gifts are being developed into God-given skills.

As children begin to read there is that marvelous time in which they are excited to read anything—billboards, boxes, and books. A school principal once encouraged a group of parents, "Listen to your child—read anything, even the cereal boxes at breakfast!"

This is the golden moment at which to give the child a Bible of his or her own. Many people ask me, "Just what Bible storybook do you recommend for children?" Even the best of them still seem to provide an unnecessary crutch. Simply give the Bible. As we read the Bible with our children, our words make the Bible clear and alive. We do not need to embellish the Scripture. Many Bible storybooks with titles like *Donkey Daniel in Bethlehem* have tried to entice children to become interested in the Bible by adding cute little parts to make Scripture more palatable. The Bible is exciting. It is clear and meets us where we are. Appropriate use of Scripture is all that is needed.

Many churches present Bibles to all second- or third-grade children. This special presentation in church is an important time. Just as the sacraments are publicly celebrated, so the giving of the Word is noted publicly.

Nancy received such a Bible. She had been in church only two weeks, but she was nine years old. Someone might say, "What a waste—giving a Bible to a new child when who knows if she will come back again?" The risk is worth it. So what if Nancy does not come back again? That fact that she received a precious Bible from some people who did not know her but cared about her speaks for itself.

But Nancy did come back. The next week she was in church and had looked up the first scripture lesson before the service began. She was prepared to hear the public reading of the Word, and now she was able to read along. The Bible was already familiar in her hands, for, as she confided in me, "I read Genesis this week, and I'm still going!"

Industrious upper elementary children

Another little boy found the *last* book of the Bible interesting. Before going on a car trip he said, "I'm going to read Revelation again." Little was said. No testing, no quizzing. In this case, not even any discussion, except for one question, "What is it you like in the book of Revelation?"

"The seven churches," was his ready reply. There would be time years later for discussion of the cryptic meaning of all those exciting words. At this age he took delight in reading, and that was enough.

Cooperation and communication between teachers is essential in building Bible-study skills. One fourth-grade teacher said, "After the first couple of weeks the third grade didn't use the Bible again all year. Now I have the children, and it's like starting all over."

114

Another teacher said, "I want to know what ability the children have. What can I count on as the children come to me in the fourth grade?"

Consistent use of the Bible in classes is essential. As children are encouraged to underline in their Bibles what they have found to be important, the Bible becomes their own source to which they can refer again and again.

The children will continue to bring their Bibles with them to Sunday school and church if the teaching staff consistently encourages it. An extra supply of Bibles in the classroom then becomes unnecessary. In fact, a classroom Bible may be a distraction because it is an unfamiliar tool. "In my own Bible I know where I left off," says Jan. "In the Bible in Sunday school I can't find my place."

The child who grows to use the Bible inductively will grow to love the Bible. From such curious searching and reading will come questions. The class is a partner to the children's individual skill building. Enforced drill is no substitute for the familiarity which comes from personal search and discovery.

The classroom is a place for talk about the format of a Bible. One young boy had discovered much on his own and told me, "If I don't know where to find something in the Bible, I just turn to the table of contents, like you do in library books." Children might ask, "What is a chapter? Why are there verses? Wouldn't it take less time to find things if we knew the books of the Bible in order?"

Erikson's industry vs. inferiority stage is significant at this age. A child delights in "being able" to read, to list, to find, to know. Those Bible baseball games do build skills and are part of the total educational picture—but as a means to an end. The child who memorizes the books of the Bible but never discovers the excitement of reading the Bible on his own has a skill and nothing for which to use it. The child who delights in memorization games to the end that Scriptures are familiar friends has honed a skill for lifelong use.

And then come the questions, "Where does the Bible come from?" "Why are there four gospels?" "Who wrote Proverbs?" Books about the Bible are helpful at this point.[13]

Some people ask, "What translation of the Bible should children have?" That is something the teaching staff and educational committee of the church should talk about together. What a great opportunity to really read and dig into the various Bible translations in order to make that decision knowledgeably! For the upper elementary school child I choose the Revised Standard Version with concordance.

Searching teens

For the teenager I select the Good News Bible. Why the simpler translation for the older student? Because the vocabulary ten-year-olds use is more extensive: they like to explore vocabulary. Adolescents have moved to Erikson's identity vs. identity diffusion stage. No longer intent on learning new words, they are now self-conscious in front of their peers. Teens will be careful *not* to display all the words they know. The teenager needs a translation which is matter-of-fact, down-to-earth. The pocket-size version of the Good News Bible is great for teens. I have said to seventh-graders, "I hope this version of the Word of God can become as comfortable to you as your favorite pair of jeans. You can slip into it. It feels right. You know who you are in it." Now they have two translations which they can compare. The teen who has had the

Bible as central in his Christian education will continue to place it there. The translation may change, but the Word grows and meets him again, always where he is.

As class began, a group of teenagers were talking about the soap operas they watch after school every afternoon. I was tempted to say, "Is that what you do in the afternoon? What a waste of time! We might as well keep you in school longer." Instead I joined them where they were and heard them relate what had happened to Jessica and how Bob had carried on and where Bill and Angie were in their affair.

"Do you know there is something like that in your Bible? Look up 2 Samuel 11." They did and they read! We talked for a while about it, and then quite willing to lay it aside lest the students think I was just baiting them, I said, "Well, let's go on to. . . ." I was interrupted by one girl, "No, let's read on. How did it come out?" We read on and learned how covering up one problem led to another, deception to self-deception. We read Nathan's words to David and David's repentance, and then Psalm 51.

Almost any section of Scripture is rich with meaning for life. One high school Bible class spent almost a year on the book of Genesis and found out the 12 sons of Jacob had a sister. They pondered the meaning of Hagar and Ishmael in the history of the world's religions. They waited with Jacob as he wondered and worried about meeting Esau again after so many years. They felt the jealousy of Joseph's brothers. They waited with the brothers when Benjamin's sack was found to have the missing cup. And they laid Israel to rest in the land of Canaan, and knew the ominous future of the children of Israel in Egypt. This was only the beginning of the story.

All of human emotion and adventure is found in those

117

pages of Genesis. We shared much along the way. We shared world events, personal worry and waiting, family jealousy, and reunion. The journey was long but good.

Into adulthood

Another method of inductive Bible study, one which has promise for upper elementary through teens and into adulthood is word study. It involves search. It involves erasing preconceived ideas. Word study is searching the Scriptures for concepts which give meaning to those who search.

In four one-hour sessions one group studied *W* words. A group of adults used a concordance to study the word *way*. Working as a group, people began by setting aside preconceived ideas about *way* and then set out to see how that word is used in the Old and New Testaments. Individuals studied particular references, asking, "What does the word mean in regard to God and God's people in this instance?" After each person had worked alone, they brought together their research. Only after the thorough searching did the small group summarize this concept, now rich with meaning: After the fall God placed in the garden an angel with a flaming sword that guarded the *way* to the tree of life. But later God led his people in the *way* through the wilderness. God's people walked in the *way* of the Lord. People followed in the *way*, but God also sent people on their *way*. Finally Christ declared, "I am the *way*," and the Christians in Acts were called people who belonged to The *Way*.

They went on to study more *W* words, like *water, wind, waste, watch, walk, wheat, woman,* and *womb*.

Children can begin to use a concordance, not just to look up a passage they can't find, but to begin to explore connections in the Bible, letting Scripture interpret Scripture, developing a sense of continuity of God's working with people.

A group of teenagers did a word study on the word *flesh*—well aware of the "skin-flicks" of our day. They began searching through Scriptures, beginning with Genesis, "And they became one flesh." They studied the sacrificial meaning of flesh, clean and unclean, the wasting away of flesh. Finally, after much searching and sharing, they came away with a new sense of awe for the words of St. John, "And the Word became flesh and dwelt among us."

In word study it is not just the summary of the concept (one could go to a Bible dictionary for that), but the search itself that is so rewarding.

The central concern in inductive, skill-building learning is that the method be congruent with the goal. One can use crossword puzzles, or Bible baseball as well as word study. But what learning activities match the age level? And are these learning activities appropriate to the learning goal? For example, a crossword puzzle is good for an 11-year-old when the goal is to become acquainted with the names of the minor prophets. Crossword puzzles would be inappropriate for teenagers learning to understand the concept of "real presence" in Holy Communion. Because they are learning to think abstractly and are concerned with their own identity as separate from the faith of their parents, they need learning activities which lead them in the midst of their daily searching.

An inappropriate learning activity is "scripture pills," in which a child takes a small piece of paper with a Bible verse on it, from a small capsule. This method conveys the concept that Scripture can be swallowed in daily doses to increase happiness. A better way to help people learn to use and love the Bible is to encourage personal growth in ability to use the Scriptures devotionally and for personal search.

To study the Bible inductively is to be led into the riches of God's Word in such a way that each student, at whatever developmental stage, grows in knowledge, grows in understanding about God, and grows in new skills to ready each for the next learning stage.

Chapter 5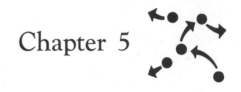

Individualized Learning

The child had been abused and was not easily going to allow any new adult to touch him. From time to time in those two weeks one would see the older crafts teacher, sitting in a book nook in the narthex, reading to her new young friend.

The last few years we have seen a growing interest in educational styles which could be termed *Individualized Learning.* Some congregations have tried the creative, but demanding route of open classroom, perhaps mirroring the exciting new face of open education in the public school. Others have discontinued their church's published curriculum in the promise that independently produced individualized learning packets would cure confirmation-class discipline problems.

Individualized learning considers the person, which lecture style and even group activity education often do not. But no one style of education will prevent or cure discipline problems. A student's behavior (termed *problem behavior* or *poor discipline* when it does not meet the expectations of the teacher) is a signal. The student is saying something—about himself, about the learning environment, and about the material to be learned. Reading those signals clearly can help us design educational ministry programs. But even a program designed for the individual will not guarantee that the student will learn or that there will not be problems within the learning community.

People learn *in* groups, but one person does not think, conceptualize, conclude, apply or create at identically the same moment or in identically the same way as any other human being. When two people begin to say the exact same thing at the very same time, we consider it unusual. Even when a group of people is engaged in the same activity—listening to a sermon, doing a worksheet—what goes on in each person's mind is a unique and incredibly complex phenomenon. A person learns as an individual.

Conformity as control

Teachers have often denied the fact of individual learning by designing group activities that demand conformity of learning style and rate. Why? Because such training produces the effect the one who is in control desires. Because such "teaching," or training is easier. Because it enables the teacher to keep track of what is going on. It is orderly, and it enables the teacher to maintain control.

Teaching methods which expect conformity have been widely used. Often they have been labeled "introdoctrination," because people are exposed to one set of values,

122

one pattern of thinking, one set of facts, and are expected to believe and behave in one way.

While rigid indoctrination limits the variety of God's good gifts, the Christian community will want to set the parameters of belief and teaching. That is what defines a faith community. And because we have a transcendent God who has been revealed to the believing community, the individual is dependent on the faith community for that revelation. But strict indoctrination of narrowly defined facts and life-style may restrict not only God's people, but God's Spirit.

Group teaching is certainly easier than individualized instruction. To follow and control the learning of other people simultaneously is extremely difficult. But there is a fallacy here. The teacher does not need to know everything the student is thinking or learning. And there is a danger that the teacher thinks she can or should control the learning process of another person. God knows, and God is in control. Remembering that frees teachers to free people for learning.

Conformity produces comfort, at least for a while, but it denies the many-faceted gifts a creative God has given to human beings. Those people—with gifts denied, with questions unanswered, energy untapped—often finally break through even the smallest cracks in a closely regulated society and try once again to be the creative individuals they were made to be.

When I was a student teacher in a first-grade class, the supervising teacher was going through the ritual of daily penmanship class. The children were instructed to make on their lined papers a row of tall poles, preliminary to writing such letters as b, k, and l. They were to follow this with a row of short poles, necessary for such lowercase letters as i, m, and n.

Cheryl, not yet intimidated by such group learning activities, said, "I would not like to make tall poles today; I would like to make an elephant!"

The wise teacher responded, "I would like you to finish one row of tall poles and one row of short poles, and then I would enjoy seeing what elephants you can draw!"

Perhaps a more daring teacher would have said, "That's a marvelous idea! Let's all make elephants today." But even such creative teaching could impose a subtle type of conformity, assuming that every child in the room would rather make elephants than develop the skill of drawing straight lines. Or, a teacher might respond to the child's initiative, inviting others to join in, only to slip back to uniformity with a not-so-subtle, "Let's all remember to color them gray."

People are gifted with a remarkable range of interests, attention spans, skills, rates of learning, within the general range of developmental stages. They also have energy and ability to let that be known to those entrusted with the responsibility of nurturing their growth. We need to ask, How do students express those differences within our educational program?

Opportunities and options

Individualized learning can be carried out in several ways. One way is to design a classroom in which each person chooses and takes responsibility for her own learning. Students are then engaged in many separate activities.

Another way is to incorporate the awareness of individual learning needs into the large group setting.

Open-space or open-classroom education focuses on learning centers. Some schools may respond to student

124

initiative, while others have teacher-defined activities at the centers. The "openness," then, is not necessarily content, but freedom to move about the room, from center to center.

Others define individualized learning as relating primarily to time. Students complete a standard series of teacher-designed learning packets at their own pace.

While quite different, each of these styles has been termed individualized learning.

British infant schools

After a four-year study by a Parliamentary Commission, the 1967 Plowden Report announced the profundity of change that had taken place in British schools since World War II throughout England—in pastoral Oxfordshire, coal-mining Yorkshire, the slums of London and Bristol.[1] Children now arrived early, and were reluctant to leave. They initiated activities, moving from project to project—raising animals, measuring the school year, drawing, writing, dancing. The curriculum was life-related, subject to change with life as it occurred at the moment.

Such informal education and the wholistic view of teaching and learning is usually spoken about as the "integrated day." The teacher's role is to foster individualized learning which develops out of each child's particular interests. *How* the child learns is of as great an interest to the teacher as *what* the child learns. There is no testing, no competition, unless the children initiate a game which involves competition. The teacher loves, affirms, watches, and notes each child's progress, engaging him or her in conversation about activities, pro-

125

viding materials or experiences for the development of the child's ideas.

> The underlying assumption of informal schools is that in an enriched and carefully planned environment that supports the natural drive toward learning, children are able to learn in encounters with the things and people around them, and they do so at their own irregular and individual pace.[2]

The motivation is the child's own curiosity and drive to learn, truly a gift of the Creator. The assumption is that people will indeed engage in purposeful activity, in cooperation with other students.

> Four girls help their teacher, a young woman with a warm smile, to set up an exhibit of pottery just inside the front door. They are matching the browns and grays of the pots with bits of cloth dyed last week by their class. "Look, Valerie!" says the teacher, "here's what your mum finished in pottery class last night." Valerie smiles, takes the bowl carefully, and holds it up for others to see ("Oh, lovely"). She finds a place for it on the table and agrees to work with her friend Helen on a sign that will explain the exhibit. They run off to their class to get started.[3]

The Christian educator can quickly imagine the problems inherent in education that is strictly child-centered. The child is as likely to say "That pot stinks" (meaning, "It's not nearly as good as mine") or to disagree with Helen about the sign that should be made.

While recognizing the weaknesses of an educational philosophy which assumes that a person's natural curiosity will provide continuous motivation to engage in purposeful learning activities, uninterrupted by selfishness and animosity, we can note the strength of the British infant system: the emphasis is not on the teacher but on the learner, who, accepted and affirmed as an individual, will develop his or her own way of learning through discovery in relation to life.

American innovations and resistance

Educators, parents, and taxpayers have debated whether or not the American version of open education really carries out the earlier intention of the British infant schools. New buildings have been constructed (some already closed) and headlined "the school without walls." Perhaps because open education looks so different, it has been treated both as savior and as scapegoat.

In the United States many public schools have been built with an open space in the center, frequently called a learning center, a place for resources, students working with books, tapes, films, and classrooms opening out from this space. Other schools are built with large rooms in which perhaps 120 children with five or six teachers use the space for small- and large-group work as well as individual projects, moving throughout the space during the day.

Other endeavors have begun with a system, rather than an architectural plan. The Bank Street College method of open-space education has been effectively used in many communities, including inner-city schools in old buildings with contained classrooms. Here learning centers are established within the rooms, or a combination of rooms, even using the hallways in between.

Some school systems have adopted the open-space concept throughout the system, while others have some traditional schools as well. Administrators realize that not all teachers work effectively in open education.

In some communities controversies arise. People, caught in the fear that their children are not being adequately educated, often assume that children in neat rows with the teacher at the front of the room will assure a "return to the basics" and produce capably functioning, literate children.

Christian congregations, meanwhile, have watched the public school innovations. Faced with low student interest, they sometimes have assumed naively that learning centers where children and adults can choose to make a banner, compose a song, or view slides of foreign missions will ensure sustained high interest and growth in attendance.

While open education will not automatically solve the problems of discipline, motivation, declining enrollments, those who have seriously tried individualized instruction have made some exciting discoveries. But all agree it takes a tremendous amount of planning, hard work, team effort and ongoing openness and creativity.

In congregations the excitement of such a challenge has compensated for the amount of work it takes. Some have tried open-space education for a particular Sunday or for a month, following a theme such as "Old Testament Characters." Others have designed summer open-space programs. Such congregations are saying, "Our program and building must be a reflection of the life of a people, the family of God's people who join together for celebration, learning and service." [4]

While many congregations regret that all that they have is one room, large, noisy fellowship hall, this space may be the beginnings of open-space education. How can the people of God and the place in which they come together create a learning environment?

Developing individualized learning concepts

Recognizing that every person does not learn in the same way and that the Christian congregation is a group of people and a place where open education can happen, we must still identify the needs of the people of God entrusted to our care. One cannot assume that a "good" style will be good for a certain child in a certain time. The British infant schools demonstrated how a joyful, warm, exciting free experience, could replace the drab and dull repetitious rigor of the previous system. What are the needs of the children in your community today? Is there a need for open activity and more choice? Or do our children need to be freed from a bondage of choice? Do they need security, continuity, a disciplined way of approaching life so that they might develop self-discipline? Determining the needs of the learners is an important first step.

The Christian community is well equipped for effective individualized learning. First of all, each person has been individually created and gifted by God. Each also has disabilities. In the economy of a gracious creator God, each is to be valued as a child of God.

Secondly, the Christian faith radiates from a center, the gospel of Jesus Christ. Growth, success, usefulness are not measured by achievement tests. A Christian's greatest achievement is already given in Baptism. Growth is initiated by God, in a personal relationship.

While public schools argue over whether or not algebra should be taught on an individualized basis, we realize that Christian truth does not need to be acquired in a linear or cumulative way. God can begin at any point. Using the Word and sacraments and all of creation, God continues to encounter a person in the law and gospel where that person is now. Growth is from God—to God.

Thirdly, open education and individualized instruction depend on much one-on-one work. A Christian congregation is full of people, not all of whom are comfortable in "the front of the room" in formal teaching situations. But many people with a variety of life experiences can share how God has been at work in their lives. The differences among congregation members is itself an advantage. To be sure, this strange collection of individuals probably would not have chosen to be together had they not been called together by God to work in this place as a congregation. Such contemporary saints might indeed be the learning center from which other young Christians discover the faith lived in Christian vocation. Others will be facilitators, communicators, helpers, planners. Children and adults alike can be engaged in helping each other develop their curiosity about God and God's world and can be aids and resources to one another.

At a recent family camp, Doris, an adult with some writing and publishing experience, met a young boy who had just written his first story. Despite their difference in age, the two spent the next hour together. Much unprogrammed learning took place.

As a congregation plans how to use individualized learning concepts in its educational ministry, they will want to look at the Christian home as one place where such an individualized approach can happen all the time. There is time. There is continuity of relationship. There is love. Christian parents might help one another look at their home as an open space, full of learning centers where children, loved and respected, grow according to their own interest and gifts.

Individualized and community learning

While aware that individualized learning is going on all the time, the Christian congregation will be hard-pressed to structure all of its learning activities on an individualized basis. Volunteer organizations have a large potential for people to serve, but overall planning and consistency are easier to achieve in an institution where salary obligates one to certain regular performance. Individualized learning involves more adults, not fewer, more planning, not less. Spontaneous student-initiated learning will have little educative value if trained adults are not prepared to build on that experience. Plans, learning centers, materials, all kinds of resources will be needed. Teachers may be less visable, but more people will be working, planning, assuming responsibility, facilitating others in their learning.

Developing independent, individualized learning skills is a valuable tool for life. There is also need for coming together, for sharing, for talking, for discovering from another what a person cannot possibly discover through working alone.

A healthy blend of individualized learning and community learning was observed in a Christian day school. An eighth-grade class, meeting in a rather small room with few windows could have seemed drab and overcrowded. When entering the room, one was struck by the fact that each of the desks was facing the wall. Around the room all one could see were the backs of heads. Were they all being punished, made to "sit in the corner"?

As one watched, one noticed the room was bright, with good lighting, colorful with stimulating media on walls. Most significantly, there was a quiet, busy tone to the room as children worked independently, each in his or her own learning space. Later they would leave their own space and come together in a group in the middle of the room for debate, discussion, and sharing.

The home and the day school combine periods of individualized learning and learning in community. The planned educational classes of the church school, however, most often meet only one or two hours a week. Rather than using this time to be "alone" together, the Christian congregation would do well to consider the time people are apart from each other as a time of learning as individuals. The hour or two together is a precious time to be *together*, to discuss, share, and reflect on the independent learning that has gone on all week.

The time factor: contracts and packets

Most of the testing which goes on in public education is time testing. How much can you demonstrate you know in a specified and allotted time? Actually, the amount of time it takes to learn something may not be directly related to how well one learns it. The very term "slow learner" betrays our bias. While IQ may determine how quickly one can learn new ideas and how much, workers with retarded children remind us that many more people than we think can learn a specific skill, grasp a certain concept, if given enough time and patience and love.

One particular form of individualized instruction deals not so much with space as with time. Teachers have found ways to allow children to learn at their own rate through negotiation of learning contracts. The student works with teacher-designed learning packets. As one level is completed, the child goes on to the next. Any teacher who has struggled with the question, "How do I keep the three children busy while the rest of the class is still doing the work?" and "What about the child who needs ten minutes more than any other child in the group?" realizes that time should not be a barrier to effective learning.

Likewise, what message do we convey when we reward a child with free time for doing work fast? Some adults do not know how to accomplish work without the monitor and motivation of a clock, for that is how they have been schooled. Fast means good! The child quick to finish may be given "busy work," which rarely stimulates a child to work for excellence at his or her level. If all else fails, the teacher makes the child the errand person or helper. Perhaps it was the slower child who really needed the repetition of busy work and the recognition that being a helper can bring.

Learning packets are not actually individualized learning in the sense of the British infant school—a child experiencing life, being motivated to learn what and when and in what way that initial experience led her. Actually packets may be quite restricting, with time the only variable. The child can work at her own pace, but must complete the packets eventually and is quite aware from a wall chart recording the number of packets completed that she is behind or ahead of another child. Competition is not reduced.

Christian Education Media is one example of this approach to individualized learning. The objectives are characteristic of individualized instruction: the student is to proceed at his or her own speed; to use the method which suits him or her best; to spend more time with the unfamiliar, less time with the familiar; to delve into particular areas of interest without disrupting the class patterns or schedule; to use his or her interests and talents to express learning; to relate to the instructor on a one-on-one basis; to experience success; to compete with himself or herself rather than with the entire class.[5]

This program is popular not because it develops the individual interests of the child from life experience, but because the packets present an overview of Bible history, something currently lacking in many curricula. The energy required to set up the resource center and engage sufficient adults creates the challenge and excitement to carry the program for a few years. It recognizes the necessity of students working at their own pace, the one-on-one teacher-student relationship, and Bible history, but, may be disappointing because it still fosters competitiveness, rewards those who finish early, and requires teacher evaluation of set materials to be learned.

The originators state that such individualized learning must be coupled with planned community learning. A congregation should not adopt packet learning on the assumption that all discipline problems will be solved.

On the contrary, a congregation's developing its own resource center—taking into consideration the different needs of children in relation to time, and involving many adults in one-on-one relational learning—will enrich that congregation's educational ministry program. The key is a congregation developing its own program to meet its own needs.

The motivation factor

Although people are born with the gift of curiosity and the desire to learn, the human situation of brokenness and alienation reveal to us the rebellious, lazy side of our own nature. Even though they are given enough time and a loving environment, children and adults might *not* learn, *not* explore, *not* discover, *not* relate.

The Christian congregation should beware of trying to find the most exciting new program or the newest idea to beguile people into coming to Sunday school. Human beings continue to spoil even the best, making what is "fantastic" merely mundane.

What then about the motivation factor and individualized instruction? We remember best the learning that comes in response to our own questioning. Awakened curiosity leads a student beyond what his teacher may have planned. If a student is presented material before his own mind is questioning, he may not be motivated to learn it. Likewise, if a group situation oppresses a student's questions, motivation to learn will diminish. A student's own self-appraisal affects motivation.

One woman spoke to me about a chemistry course she had taken in high school. Years had passed, but even now as she related the story her eyes brightened. The course had been taught primarily as independent lab with one-on-one teacher instruction. She recalled how she looked forward to afternoons spent learning chemistry this way, developing a competency she had rarely known. "Whenever we were in class all doing something at the same time, I always feared that I couldn't get it, that I wouldn't understand. They gave me a nickname because I asked so many questions. When I took that chemistry course, I could spend as much time as I wanted and ask as many questions as I needed. I got an A in that course. But most important, the teacher helped me see myself as capable."

At its best individualized instruction considers the person and strives to develop independent learners. Studies have verified that even though formal schooling for adults may be completed, adults do continue to learn. For most adults, learning is self-selected, self-directed.[6]

Learning is habit forming. The child or adult who

135

learns to learn in self-directed ways and takes responsibility for that learning will not be dependent on external teaching forms, but be self-motivated in continuing ways. Self-directed learning can become a new, healthy habit.

Developing a Christian learning community that encourages individuals to become responsible for their own learning is a worthwhile goal. It enables people to facilitate one another's learning.

Case study: vacation school

Lest one think that open education, which takes seriously the interests, abilities and motivations of the individual, is impossible to achieve, let us reiterate that the goals are what is important. A creative people of God will find ways to work toward some of these goals. The congregation is a diverse lot. We begin there and build from that challenge.

One such congregation, intent on reaching out to the community, decided to sponsor a vacation church school, something they had not done for many years. The congregation had grown older. The Sunday school was small. Although there were seemingly too few able-bodied adults to teach and no one knew if any children would come, they set about the venture anyway.

Few adults were able to handle a large group of children, particularly children with different values and behaviors than the children they had raised years before. One older woman had some creative ideas about crafts, but her doctor would not let her come every day. While many adults thought they had no skills or gifts that would be useful, they noted and affirmed one another's gifts: "She can play the piano!" "He has some photography equipment!" "She used to be a teacher!" A group of 20 adults gathered to plan their joint endeavor.

But would there be any children to teach? They prayed and announced the vacation church school in the community. Forty children came, over half new to the church.

Everything was not calm and comfortable. People with different styles of working had to become a team. They needed to compromise on varying expectations of accomplishment and on noise level. But teachers and students discovered new skills. There was room for many different teaching and learning activities to be going on simultaneously.

A young man, out of work, was discovered to have a keen sense of directing outdoor physical activities with three-year-olds as well as with 13-year-olds. How fortunate that no one limited his teaching to one age level.

Two women who had worked together on many women's guild projects, planned to work with fifth and sixth graders. Only four children registered for that class, and two of those were part-time attenders. But the class was not cancelled because there were not enough children. Instead, those two adults and two students had a delightful two weeks. That special two-on-two relationship will not soon be forgotten.

Because of an informal conversation about the 50th anniversary of Lindbergh's flight across the Atlantic which had been on the news the night before, one of the teachers gave a boy a scrapbook of the flight which she had made as a school project 50 years earlier when she was his age.

In another part of the building a woman who works ably with small groups of children, amid bustling activity, supervised crafts. That room was noisy, with productive confusion, 10 or 12 children talking at once.

The retired schoolteacher also worked with a group, in her quiet, well-ordered style.

The woman whose doctor advised her to come only twice a week worked on alternate days, usually with one or two children at a time, in quiet, intensive ways.

Meanwhile, the third- and fourth-grade teacher, with her teenage daughter as helper, had a class of 12 children. While watching her own group, she noted a new child roaming around the morning chapel service. As she tried to encourage him to sit down by her, the child stiffened, bristled, and protested about being touched. Later that morning it was found that the child had been abused, and was not easily going to let any new adult touch him. From time to time in those two weeks, one would see the older crafts teacher, sitting in a book nook in the narthex, reading to her new young friend. The child now unafraid, quite comfortable with his newfound, trustworthy adult friend.

All of these learning situations were made rich by an almost unheard of ratio of one teacher for two pupils. These varied situations were held together by gathering to worship, going apart to learn in many places and many ways, by carefully scheduling, and by moving from learning activity to learning center throughout the morning. All gathered at the end of the morning for sharing and celebration.

Incorporating individualized learning

People learn as individuals and people learn *in* groups through shared experiences. But congregations do not need to limit intentional educational experiences to stereotypical groupings. In response to the tired lament, "We don't have enough teachers (or children, or space, or

138

time) to have a class," the response can be "Where two or three are gathered in Christ's name, God is present, and teaching and learning can happen." Perhaps it may even happen more creatively because the challenge of finding ways for this diverse assortment of people to teach each other is so great. A Christian congregation that begins by assessing individual needs and gifts can create an open learning community.

The term *individualized learning* seems to narrow the focus, but it can reveal to the congregation the multifold ways learning can take place in community with creative use of space, time, resources, and relationships. We need to ask, What is special about this congregation? What is the flow of life? How can the building serve as a learning center? Who are the many people?

Individualized learning means different things. It is not a cure-all. In fact, the new possibilities it offers requires greater commitment and discipline. But the adventure will be well worth it.

Chapter 6

Confrontation and Clarification

Mr. Whithers' eighth graders were wrestling, in the class-room, with the classic Christian problem, "If God is all-powerful, how can God be good and if God is good, how can God be all-powerful?" Brian could not deal with that classroom confrontation, at least at that moment. But each Christian bumps headlong into that seeming contradiction while living in the midst of the catastrophes of this world.

Most sixth and seventh graders were stricken with fear by the tales told of Mr. Whithers' eighth-grade class. His loud voice and demanding manner hid his compassionate heart. He expected results of his students and tested their endurance. He challenged their statements, forcing them to stand up for their opinion. They were confronted with opposing ideas. They were confronted with Mr. Whithers.

After young Brian had recounted his understanding of the explanation of the First Article of the Creed, Mr.

Whithers informed him, in a tone of unchallengeable authority, that God could not be both all-knowing and still care about the individual. Mr. Whithers confronted Brian with slashing questions: What about those villagers killed last week in an earthquake? Did God love them? If so, why didn't he prevent that catastrophe? Had God caused it?

Brian, overwhelmed by that probing adult voice, could not respond. When Mr. Whithers demanded he must answer, Brian felt tears coming. He wondered how he could leave the classroom to cry in the bathroom where none of his classmates would see him.

Brian made it through that class and through the year. He survived Mr. Whithers. But we're left wondering why Mr. Whithers taught that way? Did he enjoy it? Was he copying a teaching style he had experienced as a student? Did he take pleasure in being known as a "hard" teacher?

There are students and teachers who seem to thrive on confrontation and debate. For others, these are uncomfortable learning styles, perhaps even degrading. But whatever one's reaction, confrontation is a memorable teaching style. There comes a time when all that we have heard, all that we have learned, discussed, experienced, is confronted by another person, by another ideology, or by our own life-style. This may be difficult, painful, even devastating, but it is necessary.

There are benefits and limitations to this facet of learning. The children in Mr. Whithers' class survived. Some may even have grown in self-esteem as well as clarification of concepts. But what was the long-range effect? And what about the motivations of a teacher who uses confrontation as a primary style? Is the rigor for the sake of the child or for the sake of the teacher's ego?

In this chapter we shall consider from a theological perspective the Christian confronting God, the world, and the self. We shall examine the popular values clarification exercises, which force students to come face to face with their beliefs and their actions. We shall look, too, at the rationale for testing as a part of Christian education. Finally we shall sharpen the age-old tool of debate, as well as look at the educational possibilities in the conflict inherent in Christian community.

God is testing you

Values clarification and confrontation are no doubt here to stay. Actually confrontation is as old as Genesis: "Did God say, 'You shall not eat of any tree of the garden'?" and "Where is Abel, your brother?" Failure to stand fast is that old, too, for Adam and Eve ate the fruit. And there was defensiveness in Cain's response to confrontation: "Am I my brother's keeper?"

When a friend is going through a rough time, some people say, "God is testing you." But God does not test people to see if they pass or fail.

If one is going to be a Christian and live in this world, one will learn through confrontation. God is not toying with people, and we are not puppets on a string. We are change agents and care givers, empowered with new life in the Spirit. Such new life in Christ, by its very nature, is action; and action invites reaction.

Values clarification is not a substitute for Christian education. It has always been at the heart of Christian learning through everyday living in the world. The intent of values clarification is to help people clarify what they believe, and therefore what they value. This is different from a methodology which tries to persuade a learner to accept some predetermined set of values. This approach affirms the crucial importance of values, but also affirms that people can reflectively define their relationships and actions in an everchanging world.

Later in this chapter we shall speak to the question, "Is values clarification value-free?" For now we confine ourselves to the question of the relation between belief and life, and the necessity of confrontation and clarification as necessary educational processes in "learning" the Christian life.

Mr. Whithers' eighth graders were wrestling, in the classroom, with the classic Christian problem, "If God is all-powerful, how can God be good, and if God is good, how can God be all-powerful?" Brian could not deal with that classroom confrontation, at least at that moment. But each Christian bumps headlong into that seeming contradiction while living in the midst of the catastrophes of this world.

The choices we make each day and the behavior patterns which are the culminations of those choices testify to the beliefs we hold. We can benefit from clarifying what we believe when our beliefs confront the world. If these confrontations take place within a caring Christian community, we benefit from clarifying interchange with significant others.

Faith, works, and humanism

Our ability to reflect on our actions shows that God created people to think. We cannot think our way into a right relationship with God. But we are created to be reasoning people. Redemption in Christ does not change that, but frees us to use our reason in ways that no longer need to make ourselves the center of the universe. On our

144

own we do not value God or God's will for the world. In Christ we are set free to value God and the world in new ways.

Christianity is not part faith and part reason. There would be no way for us to pass God's tests, intellectually or behaviorally. Our actions are a result of faith. When our actions do not match our profession of faith, then we have a crisis of faith.

This facet of learning sharpens the point where all of that becomes clear. Do we indeed believe that God is God? Are we saying the words of the faith of our fathers and mothers and not owning them for ourselves? Do the things we have learned to confess stand up under the pressures of life?

The question is not "Do my actions show my faith?" Our actions always testify to a faith, either the faith I profess as a Christian, or faith in another god, the god of acquisition, or security, or expediency, or acceptance.

Values clarification could be said to have a humanistic base (although, technically speaking, it can be used to clarify the values of any faith). Humanism maintains that people are free to use their intelligence to determine their relationships in an ever-changing world. A Christian would say that human beings have a propensity to hide and blame and hate and therefore will not always use their intelligence to make wise choices for the welfare of humankind. But in Christ that person is free to make choices on a new base, free to love with God's kind of love, to care for the world, to act on behalf of justice with God's kind of mercy. This is a total difference of direction.

The Christian is now free to be a humanist in a new sense of the word. As Christian educators, we realize that Christian people often misuse their new freedom by doing nothing in the world, avoiding hard questions, or sitting back and smugly judging others.

This facet of educational ministry does not propose that a testing of faith is necessary as a means of winning our way to God or winning for God. It is necessary because we all live in the world. Christians who find living in the world easy may well be deceiving themselves. Moments of calm are gifts, not the goal. The goal of Christian education is that by God's grace people come to new life in Christ and that they be Christ's people in the world. Education in the confrontational and clarifying styles challenges people to do that.

Education for mission

The goal of educational ministry is not that the Christian will be comfortable in class, even though many other facets of education examined in this book call for a warm nurturing atmosphere. Education that has as its goal the comfortable life is not Christian education.

One parent interviewed as to her expectations of the church's youth educational ministry program replied, "Teach my child the Christian faith so he won't get into trouble." Another said, "Teach my child so that I won't have to worry about him growing up in this world." A Christian's faith and life will not be guaranteed safe, even if he or she attends Sunday school every Sunday for 52 weeks or for 52 years. But *God* is safe and trustworthy, and God will not allow Christians to be tempted beyond their strength.

Christian education is for mission, for engagement with the world. There is a rhythm to this style of learning. Some might picture it as advance and retreat. That warfare imagery, quite prevalent in Christian hymnody, is questionable. We are not, after all, out to conquer the world nor really even to conquer the world for Christ. Was that the mode of the Master Teacher?

Rather the rhythm of this style of learning is seen in God's people historically: "Separation and mission are two aspects of the call to be a witnessing community. The goal is a world reconciled with God." [1] The child of God is held lovingly in the hands of God, but still lives in the world and will be tempted by his own self and by other gods. Our teaching needs to equip this child for such confrontation. The purpose of Christian education is to equip the Christian community to be in the world—speaking the Word in love, acting with mercy and justice. We need not back away nor protect our children, but stand with them, praying and encouraging as they begin to stand in their faith and act on their faith.

The Christian learner—child or adult—is growing in wisdom and reason and the ability to make choices and act. This is not in order to "decide for God"—because God has already decided to love this person. This facet of learning is not a competitive activity for its own sake, but is a mark that the Christian learner is now alive and thinking and walking in this world.

Values clarification

Christians have often been charged with hypocrisy, but no one sets out to be a hypocrite. Living a faith life in a complex world is difficult. Some people know what they believe, think clearly about their decisions, and act decisively. They do not merely adjust to life, but approach life purposefully, acting from their beliefs and often causing significant change in the world.

On the other hand, many people, perhaps a growing

147

number because of the complexity of our society, are not clear about how they relate to people and issues. They may "know" quite a bit. They understand the concepts and components of the faith they profess, but are behaving out of quite a different faith stance. Their behavior is apathetic, flighty, uncertain, inconsistent. They may become drifters or overconformers, or they may become overdissenters, no more independent than the overconformer.

A young man professes a basic tenet of the Christian faith: that he fears and loves God above all things. Actually he fears and loves many things more than God. He fears his job supervisor. He is afraid of losing his job and thereby not being thought of as an adult by his peers. He loves a sense of independence and aquisition of his new car. He cares about the well-being of others but finds it difficult to love his neighbor as himself when that neighbor is vying for his job promotion.

Free choice

Values clarification is one model of bridging the gap between belief and action, one style of teaching that fosters priority setting and choice making. Changing mores and complex societal structures challenge the Christian who wants to make decisions within a framework of thought which expresses the new life in Christ.

What is free choice anyway? Throughout history human freedom was rare. Now we have come to a time of relative physical comfort and economic independence as well as vocational and geographic mobility in which "freedom of choice" has almost become a burden. We seem incapable of making the choices before us: "Which job shall I take? Which school shall I attend? Which person shall I marry? Shall I marry at all?"

God has given us the ability to comprehend and decide, but at times our life seems so complex that the process is almost overwhelming. Freedom of choice has become bondage of choice.

Helping people clarify their actions and the ramifications of those actions is important: "What do I believe, and what are the implications of that belief for my life in the world?" For the Christian the new life in Christ means freedom from false gods and false priorities. The Christian is free to value life in a new way, but the Christian also needs to think through what such new life in Christ means. Values clarification helps the Christian learner—child or adult—clarify what values his actions display and what belief systems are working behind those values.

There are three parts of valuing: choosing, prizing, and acting.

Choosing
1. A value is freely chosen.
2. A value is chosen from alternatives.
3. A value is chosen after careful thought of the consequences of each alternative.

Prizing
1. A value is cherished. One is happy with the choice.
2. A value is prized enough to be publicly affirmed. One is proud enough of a value to make it public and has no desire to hide it.

Acting
1. A value is acted upon, not just talked about.
2. A value is acted upon repeatedly. It is a pattern of life.[2]

Using and creating clarification exercises

There are many different exercises in values clarification, including *voting, ranking, continuum, either/or, listening, dilemma, interviewing,* and *goal setting.*

Voting involves a series of statements or questions to which participants respond by agreeing or disagreeing. It gives each participant a chance, without talking, to take a stand and to note the responses of the rest of the group. Whereas in the discussion only a few may speak, in voting everyone confronts the issues and takes a stance.

Ranking presents three or more possible choices for participants to rearrange in their order of preference. Ranking helps people consider a number of options and set priorities.

The *continuum* exercise presents two opposite choices of viewpoints. Respondents select that place in the continuum which most closely represents their personal view. This exercise permits a wide range of views and allows others to be at a different place on the continuum.

The *either/or* exercise is a forced choice between two options. People are often forced to make such either/or decisions in real life. In these exercises, however, the either/or is set up metaphorically, for example, "Which are you more like—a hardwood floor or wall-to-wall carpeting?" This gives opportunity for the action of clarifying and decision in preparation for life's choices.

The *listening* exercise consists of a stimulus statement or paragraph to which each person in a group of three responds individually while the other two listen. The content is controversial. This encourages those who might ordinarily keep silent to express their opinions and assures a thorough hearing of their views.

A values *dilemma* is a story that presents a dilemma but

stops short of the solution. This gives practice in generating alternative solutions and considering the possible consequences of each.

Whereas many of the earlier exercises are brief (3-5 minutes), the values *interview* consists of questions asked of a volunteer from the group. In an interview of 15-20 minutes the volunteer shares information about self, thoughts, feelings, and attitudes.

Goal setting helps translate ideas into planned action. It helps individuals to act on a decision. An individual asks others from the group to help hold her accountable for her intentions.

One can either take exercises from a source book and adapt them or develop one's own. After reading and using exercises produced by others, one could know which exercises work best with a particular group of students and learn to create new exercises as a need arises.

Life sometimes has its own values-clarification exercises. Being part of a political caucus in an election year is like taking part in one big values-clarification activity. While voting illustrates the valuing activity of *choosing*, participating in a caucus illustrates second: one must *prize* one's choice of candidate enough to act publicly on that choice. Every four years Iowans in their caucuses go through this ritual. As people come into the room, it is much like any other meeting, with eyes on the leader in front of the room. But then comes the time to physically move to a part of the room to indicate the candidate of your choice. Heads are counted. One sees one's neighbors on the other side of the room. Will this affect the relationship? Even though one felt unsure about the choice of candidate at the outset of the meeting, the place to which one has moved speaks for itself and all can see.

151

Clarification as a teaching component

Value education can be a component of other subject matter. In fact, some maintain that this is the best use of values education.[3] For example, one could study church history, learning facts about the era of the Crusades. Then one could deal with the concepts of war/holy war, land/holy land, commitment/movement. The class could try to understand how a whole community of children could be led into battle to regain distant lands they had never seen.

Then one could move to the values level, "Have you ever felt so caught up in a movement or a cause that you joined the group and became an avid follower?" One might use *either/or, interview,* or *voting* to examine the "crusading" attitude at work in our present-day activity.

Clarification is an essential facet of any Christian education class. When we are confronted by issues, we often have little opportunity to plan carefully and research options. When the school board decides to close our local elementary school, how will we react? When tax reform produces unjust benefits, what will a Christian committed to justice and mercy in the world say or do? Are we God's chosen people or God's frozen people? Are we really powerless in this world, or have we simply not learned how to clarify and translate beliefs into action?

There is of course a risk in taking this seriously. Commitment to the gospel may lead two individuals to decide quite differently on an economic issue or a foreign policy matter or even on a local zoning ordinance. The Christian community was not meant to be a safe place of inactivity. We need not be afraid of our differences. It is a community of caring people bound together in Jesus Christ, gaining strength not from their likemindedness, but from Word and sacraments which enables them to act decisively and to live in the tension of differences knowing their security and community is in the Lord. A healthy Christian learning environment can provide even the safety needed to learn to disagree and act on the opposing viewpoints.

Is values clarification value free?

There are some questions about the use of values clarification which we have put aside until now: "Is there a professed value in values clarification? Is it really value free? Is not "value free" actually a value?"

Perhaps some teachers and students believe that one is free to hold any value, no matter what the cost to others or to the society at large. But such teaching would lead to anarchy. Free to hold any values, human beings might value themselves and their own comforts above all else.

Most proponents of values clarification, however, say that the goal is not to have value-free teaching.

> We do not believe that teachers should "teach" their values to students. This does not mean you must be free of values or have a value neutrality . . . you have values . . . share them with your students. However, the teacher's values ought to be seen by student as possible alternatives, not as the only correct values. By showing students that values are an essential part of your life, you can validate the entire valuing process for them.[4]

Sidney Simon, one of the leading proponents of values clarification, holds definite values. In a speech to college students he told of his own adherence to values of physical health.[5] He eats only certain foods; he does not smoke or use beverages containing drugs—including coffee and tea. He even posts a sign outside his door that there shall be no smoking inside his home. He explains he is choosing his values and acting upon them, realizing the cost, even in the possible loss of friends.

Public schools have used values clarification extensively in recent years. In a society which is confused about values, we turn to the public school to clarify our values for us. But in a pluralistic society like ours we cannot depend on the public school to do the job of faith communities. Adult men and women, knowing their faith and acting on it, impart values to their children. The public world and the public school become a place where we learn to live safely together, with our differing values.

The goal of values clarification is not total openness but commitment. Are we able to tolerate a pluralism of commitment within our land? What is the framework within which values-clarification strategies can be helpful to the Christian community? We need not be afraid to teach the tenets of our faith boldly. We need not apologize for dogma or be hesitant in stating and living our faith. Strong convictions can provide a secure foundation in Christ so that Christians can be open to ideas different from their own.

Confrontation-education styles

Three other educational methods come under the category of confrontation and clarification: *testing, debate,* and *conflict.*

The purpose of testing

The test is prominent in education. When entering a classroom, the students are quick to ask, "How many tests will we have?" Some students develop an inordinate fear of tests and flee the classroom, become sick on test day, or drop out of college during finals week.

154

Perhaps it is the finality of testing which makes it so frightening. And some teachers, doubting their own abilities and authority, use testing as a weapon to instill fear or to motivate work—an improper use of testing.

Testing has its place when thought of in terms of healthy confrontation. In the inductive skill-building facet of education, self-testing is a guide along the continuum. In the confrontation facet of learning, the student confronts *ideas*. A mere confrontation of personalities ("I'm going to beat that mean teacher") only escalates hostility, but testing of our mental constructs, our logic, our knowledge in preparation for meeting the world is entirely appropriate.

The teacher should construct tests so that the students come away from the test knowing things more clearly than when they began. Such skills as *synthesizing* and *application* are as important to testing as *recall*. We should test not only to determine whether a student can "regurgitate" information. We should test to see if it is really theirs to use in new ways.

Testing can develop critical thinking, sharpen and focus what people know, and help students sort and weigh facts and concepts. In an effective test our knowledge is confronted, and our understanding is tested. Such testing is not a threat to our personhood, for our security is in Christ. Such testing is welcome, because it prepares us for using that knowledge and understanding in the world.

The sharpening tool of debate

Debate might be considered a public test. It is used by politicians whose stances are being tested by the public. It is used by representatives of public issues to test the worthiness of their ideas. Debating societies have been part of educational systems for centuries. Often debate is for debate's sake, for the excitement of competition.

Is debate still a viable educational methodology? Is it appropriate in the Christian community? There are those who seem to thrive on debate. Some approach all of life as though each relationship and potential relationship were a debate. Many males in our society have been taught to see life as a win/lose proposition, with winning being decisively better. On the other hand, some Christians are uncomfortable with debate, believing that the loving nature of the gospel precludes it.

The confrontation of debate is appropriate for clarification and sharpening of issues. Fuzzy thinking does not produce clear expression of the gospel. At whatever age level, however, debate should be used sparingly lest one become hooked on the combative style and unable to use other educational methods.

Debate is inappropriate as a way of witnessing to non-Christians. Trying to win debator's points with the gospel over someone else's belief probably means the person is trampled in the battle of words. Among Christians, however, it is useful to gather information and debate an issue of Christian ethics or public action. The goal of such debate is clarification through confrontation so that people are equipped for action.

Creative conflict and education

Christian communities are becoming more aware of conflict in the church. It has been present since our accounts of the early church in the Book of the Acts of the Apostles. But recently many books have been published on conflict management and the creative use of conflict. The consensus is that a certain degree of conflict can be helpful in the formation and continuation of life together.

Conflict may lead to considerable anxiety. Unresolved conflict can disable. But within a secure communal relationship which God creates, the identity of individuals need not be demolished. In his work on the creative use of conflict in religious education Donald Bossart draws on the work of Erik Erikson and Jean Piaget.[6]

In delineating stages of development, Erikson says that internal conflict is necessary in order to move from one stage to the next. Erikson deals with psychosocial development, and Piaget deals mainly with cognitive development. Piaget used the term "disequilibrium." In order for a person to develop from one stage to the next, disequilibrium is as important as the equilibrium that follows. Bossart points out that the utilization of the conflict is important. One must structure an educational environment in such a way that we creatively use the conflict the individual faces in moving from one stage to the next.

Such development is quite different from unhealthy random church fighting. Bossart connects values clarification with the creative use of conflict. He cites one model of the creative use of conflict in education, that of Robert Conrad. Four steps are involved: (1) *active struggle,* determining the nature and boundaries of the conflict; (2) *resignation,* use of silence or other activity to distance oneself from the conflict; (3) *insight,* openness to forgiveness and freedom; and (4) *interpretation,* a time for sharing and testing the validity of insights.[7]

A framework for confrontation and clarification

While setting people up for conflict in order to enjoy the battle is inappropriate, conflict will exist wherever human beings gather. Inner conflict is necessary to human

157

growth and development. How can Christian educators recognize and foster confrontation and conflict?

Creating a learning environment which reflects God's loving acceptance of us is essential. Consistency is a key. In order to know a trustworthy God, people must see the consistency of love and care in the Christian community. They need to know that parents and teachers and other significant mentors and peers are not going to abandon them if they dare to share the conflict they are feeling.

Within a consistent loving Christian community, teachers and students alike can be open to confrontation, honestly welcome it, and use clarifying strategies to bring the conflict to resolution.

Confrontation need not be used only by those who proudly claim it as their particular style. It can be a valuable educational method for any teacher to use appropriately—not to produce powerful winners and quaking losers, but to foster the growth of all.

Chapter 7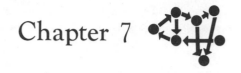

Experiential Learning

They tried with great frustration to describe the color blue. To know another's belief is as difficult as seeing through another's eyes. We can learn about another's faith as it is described to us, but we cannot see life through his or her eyes of faith.

Running into the Visual Education Center late one Friday afternoon, the youth director cried, "I need a simulation game for Sunday—any one will do. I've just got to have something! Learning has to be fun, or my class won't come. A simulation game always goes over big."

Experiential learning is fun. Role play, simulation games, and case studies join the time-honored retreat and field trip as models of educational ministry that engage the experience of the learner. The excitement of this style, however, is no substitute for goal setting, sound preparation, and compatibility of objectives and methodology. Because experiential education is powerful, it should be used with care.

Memorable, not memorized events

We remember learning events from years ago: the grade-school field trip to the local park to study deciduous trees, the first youth-group conference out of town.

We also remember the death of our father, the birth of our baby, the fire in the middle of the night, the automobile accident, the recognition dinner. These are also the substance of experiential learning. There is no need to "memorize" such events. Every minute is memorable.

Who we were before the experience shapes our action and our learning during the event. What happened, how we responded, and the relationship of others determine the meaning that experience will have for us. Our own reaction leads us to make conscious or unconscious decisions for the future. Our reflection on the experience shapes the persons we are to become.

False dichotomies

Throughout the history of the church, faith has been measured in varying ways. At times faith was validated by the emotion of a conversion experience. At other times knowledge and intellectual assent to doctrine identified a Christian; the daily lives of people were deemed less important than correct teachings about life. While the former could lead to individualistic faith, the latter ignored human experience. But God encounters the whole human being—emotions and intellect.

Church history reminds us that people have also tried to separate the spiritual from the physical. Early Gnosticism and Marcionism did not believe that Christ was truly human. Today Christians who want to keep life inside the church building, separate from the rest of the week, evade the cross and the essence of their own humanity.

But, Christ came in the body. He walked the dusty roads, talked with people in the synagogue and in the marketplace and at the well. His teachings were almost always a reflection of and a commentary on the events of daily life. Jesus' words also called people beyond themselves, so that the events of life took on deep significance.

It is not that the flesh is bad, while the spirit is good. Rather, the old nature which requires us to justify ourselves is gone, so that the new Spirit-filled life may come forth. But our new being lives here on earth. We still experience life in all its earthiness, but we see life in a new perspective and are set free for a life of service. We still have flesh and blood, we think and feel, have minutes and hours to our days. But now the Word who put on flesh, the incarnate Jesus, empowers us with the Spirit. Our Christian life is experiential, and Christian nurture takes place through life experiences.

God's people are curriculum; Christian education is mission

What does this mean for teaching and learning in the congregation? It means that life experience is more than example to illustrate a theological truth. It means that curriculum is not related to only some parts of our lives. Every dark and bright corner of existence is substance for theological reflection. God's people alive in this place *are* curriculum. All else is resource.

The curriculum is not something one purchases from a

publishing house; one buys curriculum *resources*. Educational ministry is not a compartment in the church. Nor is it a means to an end, such as church growth or congregational survival. It is not something you do to children on their way to becoming adults and therefore "real" members of the church. Nor is it a moral Band-Aid for American society, a means of producing "good" people.

Through being the church the people of God understand what that church is. Christian education is "a way we can participate in Christ's invitation to all men, women and children to join in God's mission of restoring people to their true humanity by reconciling them to God and to one another." [1]

God's people living and serving in the world are the curriculum for ongoing growth. Through engaging in outreach, children and adults learn to know how much God's love is an outreaching, all-encompassing love. At the point of involvement in ministry with all its joys and frustrations people hunger to study the Word. Relevant at last are the Acts and the Epistles, church history and a study of world religions.

Children, as well as adults, can be engaged in ministry. They can visit nursing homes or gather food for the hungry. In being the church they learn what it is to be the church. Reflection upon such experience heightens the growth potential. As one become fatigued from the work of ministry, one hungers to be nourished on the Word.

When adults or children are merely spectators to ministry or the audience for the sermon, they become stuffed and can no longer hear the Word, for it has not been lived out to the point that they hunger to be fed again. The life together of the Christian community is the essence of its curriculum and results in mission and ministry.

162

Types of experiential education

Simulation is a way of looking at and dealing with life through indirect means. Drama, in which the learners are the actors, provides an opportunity to reenact the experience of people of another time, another place. *Biblical simulation* is more than practicing for a performance. It is a way of sharing the experience of God's people. *Simulation gaming* and *role playing* enable us to see ourselves and our interactions with others. *Family sculpture* examines the way the family system in which we live shapes and forms our lives.

Real and vicarious life experiences are an important source of learning. But experience is not automatically the best teacher, for we may be so close that we overlook or distort the learning possibilities. *Surfacing experiences*, redeveloping adult curiosity, and *utilizing field trips* are some ways of building on life experiences.

Case study is a means of capsulizing a real-life situation for the purpose of looking at the entire picture through the eyes of the many participants. *Retreat* and *fantasy* are ways of living a piece of our life in a special way, breaking open new potential for growth and decision.

Experience has powerful possibilities for teaching, but it should not be given free reign in its teaching power. The importance of theological reflection on experience cannot be overstressed. James and Evelyn Whitehead suggest a tripolar approach to such theological reflection. One pole is experience. The other two poles are Christian tradition and cultural information. By attending to the information from all three sources, one can move to decision for Christian living and ministry.[2]

163

Simulation

In Chapter 1 we discussed drama as a form of presentation. In this chapter we speak of drama in which the learners are the players. Scenery and costumes need not be professional, for being in the drama is the important thing.

In one sense, acting is a hiding of our real identities. As we play a part other than our own, we hide or escape. But in another sense we reveal. Simulation is both a drama and a game. In losing ourselves in such play we may drop some of the masks we wear. When the spotlight goes on, the spotlight is, for a while, off our usual identities. In such a play we may reveal to ourselves, and to trusted others, some important aspect about ourselves.

Some Christian teachers consider intellectual learning to be more important than affective learning. Intellectual formulations and the associative and imaginative functions of experiential education, particularly simulation, come together in the split-brain hypothesis. Though developed in the early 1950s by Joseph Kamiya and others, it has become the subject of much interest in the past few years.

Scientists hypothesize that the left hemisphere of the brain, connected to the right side of the body, carries out the functions of speech, logic, cognitive reasoning, analysis, and linear activities, while the right hemisphere of the brain, connected to the left side of the body, assumes the functions of visual, artistic, imaginative, associative, and relational activities. John Westerhoff speaks about the overemphasis on theological formulation (doctrinal statements), but warns that our current enthusiasm for the split-brain concept could lead to an uncritical "experiential" emphasis. "Right lobe religion is not more healthy than left." [3]

Experiential learning, simulation for example, does not need words to be valid. But neither does experiential learning invalidate verbal expression, critical thinking, reasoning, and analysis. We need to affirm both as part of the human ability to function and to learn.

Simulation games

Simulation games may be six-hour events or two-minute experiences. There are many on the market such as *Star Power, Agenda, The Banner Making Game, Biblical Society in Jesus' Time, Gospel Game,* and *The Lovable Church Game.*[4] Some publishers provide volumes of structured experiences for human relations training.[5]

In teaching classes on simulation gaming, my husband may use such ordinary table games as Monopoly, chess or card games such as Hearts. Then he will invite the players to talk about their experiences. He maintains that games play people. When we play a role, the role begins to affect us.

In a book on simulation games Richard Reichert provides interesting simulations and guidance for teachers who want to develop their own.[6] But he sees simulation as a means to a higher end, "the end being to help students gain a better insight into particular truth, value, or evil related to faith life. . . . After allowing the students to experience the topics and to find them pleasing, the teacher can initiate more technical or detailed discussion." [7]

Experiential learning is valuable by itself. It is ironic that even an advocate of experiential learning should say that simulation is merely a way to "get into a topic" so that the teacher can teach ideas and definitions. Intellectualizing is not a higher form of learning; however, discussing the experience, in community, extends the learning possibilities and provides for us that balance of tradition and cultural information which our own personal experience needs.

Biblical simulation

By placing ourselves in a role we also learn something about another. We may learn about Joseph by reading the Bible or seeing a film or watching a play. But by doing what Joseph did, by going through the motions, we can catch nuances of meaning we never could have by sitting in a chair with legs and arms crossed.

By playing a biblical character, a person can understand himself in a new way. In playing the role of Peter as he denies Jesus—in feeling the fear, in wanting to hide and defend oneself, in denying one knows anything about that man — a person also comes face to face with his own fear and habits of denial. Then when we read the words of the angel in the final verses of Mark's gospel, "Go, tell the disciples, and Peter, he is going before you to Galilee. He will meet you there," that word of acceptance from a risen Christ comes through with new power.

Some who have spent hours rehearsing children for a Christmas pageant may wonder about the emphasis on playing the part rather than performing. Which is more important: the practice or the performance? We can illustrate with two preparations for a Christmas drama.

In the first drama the children are notified of the play they are to be in and receive a copy of the script. They are to memorize the lines and show up for rehearsal on three Sunday mornings and two Saturday afternoons. Each child learns the lines, but without knowledge of the rest of the play. Each learns the tedium of sitting quietly until the teacher comes to his or her part. During rehearsals each child is encouraged to speak loudly so everyone can hear, to stand up straight, and to be on time next week. The nervousness of the leader is communicated, as well as a sense that if Mary and Joseph and the shepherds are not done well, everyone will be angry—no doubt God as well.

In the second situation the teacher tells the story to the children, with the awe, the pathos, the joy of Luke 1 and 2. Then the teacher invites various children to "be" one of the characters. As they walk through the roles, the teacher asks such questions as, "What were the shepherds thinking out there in the fields? Can your body show how they felt at night, tired? Were they busy? Were they lonely? Now, how does that change when the angels appear?"

The teacher/director sets the learning environment, and the children become engrossed. They *do* the drama, experience the people whose lives were visited by God. They experience it many times in a number of ways, and then they share what they have done with others, not so much performing for them as reenacting with them the 2000-year-old story which has now become their own. In experiential education there is no such thing as *practice,* only repeated simulation. And they will remember the parts they played for years to come.

Role play

Role plays can be used at almost any age. It is most effective, however, with upper elementary, high school, and young adult groups. Younger children and junior-high age have developmental needs that take precedence over assuming the role of another. Young children love to pretend they are animals or grown-ups. Such play may be the response to the role modeling of significant adults.

167

For junior high students, establishing their own identity takes precedence over role playing among critical peers.

There are many possible uses of role play in educational ministry. Sixth graders might role play mother and father in decision making. In high school Bible class the students might role play public figures. The mission-evangelism committee might role play a possible calling situation.

The leader's role is important, inviting the players, setting the scene, helping others become appropriately quiet observers. How much of the situation should be detailed? A principle I use is to give the people something to "run with" but not so much that the scenario is so fully detailed and the player's own personality cannot express itself.

A typical role play may be five or 10 minutes long, and this often provides stimulus for a 15-minute or half-hour discussion. The role play itself provides powerful insight. After a brief silence at the conclusion I invite the participants to begin the discussion first: "How are you feeling right now?" or "How did you feel when she said . . .?" Then the observers can express things they noticed. Role plays are fun, but the one who is in the role play can be exposed and vulnerable. Creating and maintaining a nonthreatening atmosphere is crucial to a caring role-play environment.

Family sculpture

Closely connected with role play is family sculpture. We all come from families and have been formed by our living in families, however broken or whole. Family sculpture is a way of "looking" at that family system. Family counselors use family sculpture in therapy. Therapy would be an inappropriate classroom goal in educational ministry, but this activity can be a learning experience with goals of awareness and insight.

168

One person is invited to select other people in the group to represent her family members. The person asks the characters in the still-life drama to stand or sit in positions symbolizing her real family members. The individual also selects someone to portray herself and places that person in the sculpture. Are the characters close or at a distance from one another? Are some hanging on, leaning on, supporting others? Are the family members dependent on one another or detached and alienated in their relationships?

After the sculpture is set, the director is free to take another look and see if indeed this is the way things were. She may make comments. Just seeing her family thus portrayed often produces insight.

One young man who had sculptured his family said, "I didn't realize how far apart from everyone I have become. My brother is way over there on the other side of mother. The whole family is between us. I can hardly see him from where I am. I don't want it to be that way."

The director then invites the "statues" to talk about how they feel in this position. Frequently such brief feedback is accurate and will be helpful to the person sculpting his or her family. One young wife and mother heard from the mouth of the person playing her role, "Everyone is connected to me in one way or another. I can't move. All I can do is turn my head." The young woman responded that was precisely how she felt much of the time, but had never thought about it or seen it so clearly before.

Although we cannot change family members, we can learn about the family systems in which we live and through such insight make decisions concerning our actions and attitudes. We might say, "Even though my mother was distant and judgmental, I know I am loved by God, forgiven, accepted, worthwhile. I do not have to be bound by my past." Or, "My brother and I have never understood each other, but I'm going to give him a call."

Simulated experiences—gaming, role play, family sculpture exercises, and play—have the potential for powerful learning. We dare to come close to our real feelings, to surface them, to look at them, to react and make decisions. When this takes place in a warm Christian community— with its silence and support, its empathy and confidentiality—growth can take place.

Real and vicarious life experience

Simulation and real-life experience each have their distinct possibilities. Reichert says, "Never use a simulation when a real experience is available. For example, don't simulate an experience of the plight of the aged if it is possible to visit and serve the persons in a nursing home." However, simulation offers the advantages of objectivity, freeing us to feel through the very distance we have created.

Real life is prime material for potent learning. Unreflected experience, however, slips away (see Chapter 8, Journal Keeping). Reinforced negative learnings, repeated experience, teaches us forms of behavior which are difficult to change.

Vicarious experience through observation is usually more memorable than reading a book, but visiting a nursing home is still not the same as living in a nursing home. Even living in a nursing home for two weeks, as some reporters have done, is not the same as living there forever. Even ministering in the inner city for ten years, our family did not experience urban life in the same way our neighbors did, for our family was always free to leave. Nevertheless, visiting a prison is better than merely reading about one. Living on a farm or in a foreign country for a summer is better than merely passing through for one day.

Daily life is a profound teacher. Gabriel Moran says, "There is education to work and education by work. That is, our society prepares people for their jobs and, far from being neglected, this part of education may be overstressed. There is also education by our jobs. An attentiveness to what the job itself teaches might change the way we prepare people for their work." [8]

We might ask: What does a person learn from continuously working on an assembly line? What does a person learn from being a stockbroker or a parent? What does a person learn from living alone?

For years, the children in our home and in our neighborhood walked past burned-out buildings every day on their way to school. Although the schoolroom might have had pictures of pretty cities and rolling countrysides, our children learned about destruction and despair. Whether this made them destructive and despairing people or courageous survivors depends on how we utilized that learning environment of daily experience.

One year, through teacher strikes, staff changes, fatigue, incompetence, and personal problems, six teachers "quit" on our seventh grader and his classmates. By midyear even a Sunday school teacher had quit, and the Boy Scout troop collapsed. We saw the boys develop an attitude of "don't trust, because people will quit on you; don't care, because anything good will soon end."

What is the total learning environment of people whom you teach? The classroom, the work place, the home, the neighborhood? Do 500 neighbors live in 100 square miles, in six blocks, or in the same apartment building? How can we help people learn from their experiences? What are they learning? Why? How does the Christian gospel intersect with experience?

Young children easily share their experiences of the past week with a warm teacher, although, even for a child, some experiences will be too much to talk about. "They brought my father home drunk last night," may never be said aloud.

But how a child reacts to crisis indicates who that child is. Our three children deal with crisis in different ways, partly because of age, partly because of their distinct personalities. When riding in a car during a thunderstorm, one wanted us to hurry to our destination; another remained silent; another nervously chattered away at full speed. In response to a robbery one lashed out in anger at the robbers who took our belongings, vowing to find them; one had nightmares; one "played out" with his toys the frightening experience.

In using the substance of life in educational ministry we facilitate growth through reflection. We enable the tenets of our faith to hold us. We enable people to develop the skill of interrelating the reality of God and the reality of their daily lives. Christian education which does not encompass the real-life experiences of people is not Christian education. People may say that the church is not relevant, but God is relevant. God cares. Educational ministry should not be merely life-related, but reality-based.

Surfacing experience

Perhaps we feel it is our duty as a teacher to present the basic tenets of the faith and let the student apply them to life. Dealing with a book is so much safer than becoming involved in people's lives. In a book the discussion questions are already given, while someone in the pain of crisis frequently cannot even articulate the problem, much less find a ready solution. Is it fear that causes us to ignore the business failure or the cancer diagnosis?

There *is* safety in objectivity, and the classroom need not become a therapy group. However, the Christian learning community can establish an environment of trust into which people begin to bring the crises of life. "How was your week?" may be a simple but effective invitation. Communication may take place without giving all the details.

During a Sunday morning Bible study meeting in the sanctuary, a class pondered the meaning of Christ's humiliation in Mark 10. Quietly, with safe spaces in their togetherness they shared the pain of humiliation they personally had known. One man said only, "For me it's a feeling of being incompetent, being unable to function." People did not probe this usually self-assured man. That was enough. We received each other's experience with those few words. We spoke and listened and drew near to each other and did not even notice the gathering numbers of people coming in for the second church service. We felt the strength of the communion of saints that day.

Sometimes the experiences of life will be surfaced through an outside occurrence. A number of years ago when the popular *MASH* television series was running in prime time on Saturday nights, our high school Bible class came one Sunday morning, needing to tell me about the previous night's episode. The students detailed the entire program, chuckling as they recalled the hilarious parts. But as they recounted the conclusion, I began to see the reason for their urgency to verbalize the story. Colonel Henry Blake, the first commanding officer on the series, was ending his tour of duty. Although most of the program had been a grand, funny farewell, the epilog

173

brought word that Blake had been killed on the way home.

The teenagers were experiencing grief! Although they had seen thousands of killings on television, this was not an unknown victim, but someone they had grown to know and care about.

In that collective experience they began to talk about other grief experiences. One student said, "My grandmother died last year, and I really miss her." We were able to discuss important questions: "What is grief? What is death? What is Christ's death to me?"

Field trip

Going to another place and asking with my eyes, ears, and feet, "What can I learn from you?" invites experiential learning. Field trips have long been used in Christian education. The quality of the "going" determines the result. Purpose, plan, and participation are necessary if the field trip is to be more than a recess. If class members are not part of the planning process, they may remember only the restroom, the hot weather, or their particular seat on the bus.

I have seen simple field trips to the local library collapse because a leader forgot to check on the directions or whether the library would be open. At the same time I am impressed by the planning of the Dubuque seventh-grade field trip to Chicago. For a whole week before the trip teachers in every subject talked with students about what they would see. Then eight buses full of children, accompanied by teachers and some parents, traveled four hours to Chicago, visited the Aquarium, Museum of Science and Industry, the Museum of History, the Sears Tower, and returned to Dubuque that night, stopping at precisely 7:08 for supper. A field trip with hundreds of seventh graders could have been a disaster, but careful planning made it a valued educational experience.

Caroling to shut-ins is both ministry and experiential education. A leader needs to travel the route first, consider the timing, the needs of the people, transportation, and weather. Such planning leaves room for the element of surprise, such as the time some people for whom we sang were able to join us on our journey, or such as the Christmas afternoon when we sang at a hospital, and were invited into the obstetrics ward as well.

Field trips may not be elaborate, nor reserved only for the young and restless. Rather than taking five-year-olds on an autumn walk about the block, why not take adults outside to listen to sounds they have grown too busy to hear anymore? Or send adults or youth out alone or two-by-two to walk the streets and alleys of their town and look—simply look. What do they see that they haven't seen before?

Herb Brokering has inspired many of us to ask such questions:

> Once a woman was very bored. She was so bored she almost lost her spirit. Then someone asked her a question she could not answer. So she asked questions she never thought of. She asked strangers questions until they were her friends. She asked a tree questions until she owned it. She asked a factory questions until she knew it by heart. She asked an African violet questions until she knew how to care for it. She asked a person and he loved her. She asked a bird and it came into her tree to live. She asked the night questions and she slept well. She asked God questions and he blessed her with a curious spirit. In asking she receives.[9]

In being open enough to inquire, we also learn to respect the differences between us that must remain. To have learned that, is to learn much.

When teaching a high school world religions class, I began the year asking students to pretend that I was blind, having them describe the classroom to me. They valiantly tried to explain how they could see through the window which I felt and found to be hard. They tried with great frustration to describe the color blue. To know another's belief is as difficult as seeing through another's eyes. We can learn about another's faith as it is described to us, but we cannot see life through his or her eyes of faith.[10]

Case study

Inquiry into the experience of others heightens our awareness of our own experiences, allowing us to mark the similarities and the differences among us. It also builds skills for our being able to live with one another with understanding. A helpful learning tool is the case study (see Appendix, pp. 213-218 for sample). A case study is a write-up of an actual occurrence, written in such a way that the situation, the characters, the dilemma are clearly detailed. Only the outcome is omitted. As a group engages in doing the case, they try to discover who the people are and why the dilemma occurred.

The class uncovers all of the issues, the theological implications and possible choices. Through the process, dealing with a specific experience of a group of people other than themselves, the group is able to discuss issues and perhaps gain skills in working through future problems of their own.

Case study has grown in popularity in the past few years and is an excellent "experiential" learning methodology. At our seminary, students returning from internship write case studies, using fictitious names, and present them in small groups in a course on church administration.

Retreat

Sometimes we intentionally go away in order to experience life in another way. Some Christians make a personal retreat for a week once a year or for a day once a month. Through this refreshing experience the Christian is strengthened to once again confront life in the world. Each of us could benefit from the rhythm of retreat in our educational pursuits.

Youth retreats in our churches are not a new phenomenon, but they are new for the young people who go on retreat for the first time. Each retreat needs to be well planned and responsibly led. Without careful planning learning may indeed occur, but it may not be desirable learning. On a retreat students may experience alcohol or drugs for the first time, because the leader and group neglected to agree with each other about what should or should not be brought along.

Planning together is important, but youth need skills for planning (see Chapter 4). As students experience a new environment, experience the joy of Christian community, experience worship in a new setting, the event may well be life-changing and the memories long and good.

A number of youth programs, particularly confirmation instruction, are now designed for a retreat setting. Some churches conduct the entire program in retreat form. But one must remember that retreat is only one mode of educational ministry. Churches are once again seeing the value of broad and consistent youth ministry.

177

One year I taught confirmation instruction classes for two different churches in the same city. One church, with capable intelligent youth, used an annual retreat, combined with a series of five or six classes meeting at intervals during the year. The other church had a traditional one-and-a-half-hour class once a week. Both were using the same materials. I found that the class from the second church learned more during the year, probably because they met consistently once a week.

Retreat can be a marvelous educational opportunity for many ages. It has few limits if one has enough energy and ingenuity. There are church council retreats, family retreats, intergenerational retreats, retreats including the disabled, retreats for young parents, marriage encounters. Weighing goals and needs in relation to overall educational ministry will enable a church to make appropriate use of retreats.

Fantasy

If we can learn from what we do, from reality as it is, we can also learn from fantasy, from experiencing the reality of what is not. Fantasy sounds like a child's play —and it is. Fantasy sounds like elves and forest creatures and escape from reality, but it is more than that. Fantasy is a means of learning about ourselves, recalling our past, dreaming into God's promised future.

Guided fantasy is a valid educational tool. Again, it is a powerful method of education and should be used with care and competence. Actually we all fantasize every day. Some studies say we daydream over 50 percent of the time. It serves a useful purpose, giving relief from pressures of the day. It is a way of working out problems and a way of trying out plans for the future.

Fantasy is a way to recreate past experience in the warmth and safety of a present supportive community. If past relationships have impeded growth, we need not be bound forever by those experiences. As formative as past experiences were, recalling them and dealing with them with our present maturity, may help us actualize the freedom we have been given in Christ Jesus. (The Appendix has a sample fantasy for adult education.)

Fantasy is also a way to live into the future. Old and New Testament writers tell us of an expectation of the new in God's promised future. Part of Christian education is to know God's intended future for us and to live into that future experientially. The young child will learn of God's new life in Christ, a new life made his in Baptism, but which he will need to grow into. Fantasy is a way of breaking open new possibilities for the years ahead. We, of course, do not know the details, but we often have strength and gifts beyond those we are using.

For many years women could not think about growing older, for in our culture to be an old woman brought with it not the vision of maturity, strength, and wisdom, but merely loss of attractiveness. How exciting to use guided fantasy with a group of Christian women, imagining who and what they will be 10, 15 years from now, what they will look like, how they will be using their gifts.

Fantasy may bring frightening visions, representing our real fears. These inner fears are part of us, guiding our actions and decisions now. When we have the opportunity to take them out, look at them, they may lose their power.

Like all types of experiential education, fantasy is fascinating, partly because of its power. Experiential education has constant potential, but it must be used with care, providing time for good planning, goal setting, and time for discussion. If we provide a trustworthy learning environment, experiential education can move from mere distracting entertainment to a legitimately powerful learning mode.

Chapter 8

The Journal

Sometimes I go back and read the things I wrote when my children were growing up. I can hardly believe I felt as I did when I wrote those days, but I did. That's how I felt, and I understand it now.

Unreflected experience slips away. Remembering and working with our own past experiences provide growth possibilities. We are the summation of all that we have been, and yet we are not bound by our own histories. Are we subject to repeating the mistakes and losing insightful beginnings? Or are there ways that the past can inform the present and help form the future? How can we learn from our own story?

A journal provides the occasion for disciplined reflection. The practice of recording our days seems almost foreign to our modern culture, except for the caricatures of teenage romantic gossip "Dear Diary. . . ." But the journal, the log, the diary, actually have classic value. Much of our history has come to us through the journals of people whose lives have changed the world. Diaries, together with letters, have preserved biographical and historical information otherwise lost to us.

Why, then, is journal keeping uncommon today? Is it the fast-paced lives we lead? Is it the mechanical means we use to communicate? Is it the emphasis on the present, the instantaneous? The telephone, the instamatic camera, the computer seem to make disciplined handwritten recording of the day's events obsolete.

There is no purpose in condemning modern means of communication. In fact, one can certainly use a typewriter as well as a pen to record one's reflections. Time? Yes, journal keeping takes time. But many who have tried it find it a refreshing and enlightening exercise.

Journal keeping is primarily an individual learning style. And yet we consider it an educational ministry possibility for the Christian community. Whether or not we communicate our reflected experiences to others, the insight and growth affects our interaction with the community. We shall speak about the special significance of journal keeping for the person intentionally engaged in teaching. Then we shall speak about journal keeping for personal growth, and the way one learns from one's own writing at various developmental stages.

The journal: textbook about the learning process

We are all engaged in teaching and learning in almost every activity of life, and these life experiences can become a textbook about the learning process. Within the congregation we can invite teachers to keep a journal of their own life experiences, giving particular attention to occasions of teaching/learning.

Some may already keep a journal; others will never have tried. One way to introduce journals is to share samples of one's own journal entries, then invite the teachers to watch, listen, note, and record, perhaps in journals provided by the parish education committee.

Following are two sample journal entries of my own, written in a two-week period:

> One boy, about eight years old, was sitting by the edge of a motel pool on a hot summer afternoon. His brother, about 10, was already in the pool. After riding all day in a warm car, the boys were anxious to try the water, but the younger did not know how to swim. The elder brother did not know very well either, but they were safe enough in the shallow end of the pool with adults nearby.
>
> The three phrases I heard during the 15 minutes I watched became a liturgy of learning. The older boy would say, "Come on," an invitation to participate in life and learning, an enthusiastic assurance that the water was fine and the younger boy was welcome.
>
> Confident enough in his own skill to fully enjoy what he was doing he would call out, "Watch me!" a simple encouragement to observation. No details, no rigorous exercises, no informed commentary on what to do first and why, but rather a simple, "Watch me!"
>
> And after the younger boy would try to copy, as best he could, would come an assuring, "That's good." Affirmation!
>
> Minutes later, beginning again, play mixed with skill-building, came the same rhythmic, "Come on," "Watch me," "That's good!" There was gentleness, joy, consistency, and caring. In that repetition of invitation, observation, and affirmation, learning happened, not perfectly, not completely, but engagingly, enjoyably. The young boy made fear-chasing, confidence-building progress.

Another journal entry:

> Shortly after we moved to a new state, our insurance
> representative in this locale visited us. Having moved
> in only a few days before, we were physically fatigued
> and reaching the saturation point of new things to
> learn: stores, streets, names. That night my openness
> to new information was limited. Yet I knew I should
> understand what he was trying to tell me about life
> insurance, mortgage insurance, rates, benefits, and
> sliding scales.
>
> I listened, and asked questions. I found myself intu-
> itively using a reinforcement learning technique, ask-
> ing the agent to listen as I explained what he had told
> me to my husband, who had just joined us in the room.
> That helped and spurred my interest in this struggle
> to learn. I clarified information as I put the terminolo-
> gy into my own language.
>
> Even so, as we went on to more new information, I
> noticed myself actually shut off, close out any more
> facts. There was an instant feeling of "I'm not capa-
> ble," coupled with "I can't take in any more." In that
> moment I made the decision to let the insurance agent
> "go on without me." I sat quietly as his talk continued,
> no longer understanding.
>
> How closely that resembles the times we as students
> years ago sat in arithmetic or science classes and let
> the teacher "go on without us."

Curious teachers become insightful teachers through
reflection on the activity of daily life. Once a person begins
to notice, to observe, to listen, to reflect, a new way of
learning through journal keeping opens up.

One seminarian wrote:

> I have been extremely busy over the past two weeks,
> and my educational journal has suffered. This, how-
> ever, does not mean that I have stopped making entries
> in my head. This journal has been a good learning
> technique for a number of reasons. It has caused me

> to sit back and reflect on some of my day-to-day experiences. It has allowed me to see the number of ways I learn every day and has increased my learning through reflection and evaluation. I have caught myself sitting back and analyzing situations recently that I used to just take for granted.

Each of us will see events in different ways. A teacher may question the validity of learning about teaching from such an unauthoritative source. Certainly one's own journal observation should be weighed with evidence gleaned from educational research, but the very reason we see things differently teaches us yet more.

Volunteer teachers, rather than assuming they know more than enough, often doubt their own ability to learn through action/reflection. No one authority has all the insights. Catherine of Siena, writing to Pope Gregory XI, said, "As to authority you can do everything, but as to seeing you can do no more than one man."

We need to use the authority of seeing and then share and test it with others in a teacher's meeting. Teachers, of course, should merely be invited, not forced, to share journal entries, and perhaps without comment, except, "Thank you for sharing that." After a while someone might invite feedback comments, in which case others could pose comments and questions: "I wonder if this was also at work there" or, "Did you also observe ... ?" Such inductive learning leads to interest in deductive study of formal theories of teaching and learning.

Journal keeping for personal growth

The main use of journal keeping, and therefore the central focus of this chapter, is personal growth. It is useful for children, youth, and adults.

This learning style assumes that experience is part of the fabric of religion. Revelation and tradition come from outside the self and are communicated by word, symbol, and ritual. But experience and revelation need not be enemies. George F. Simon writes: "When experience is minimized, discouraged, revelation shrivels; when experience is accepted, encouraged, the seed of revelation will germinate and sink deep roots." [1]

To be a means of personal growth, journal keeping needs to take place within a relationship with the living God. Left to our own resources, we either will believe that the world revolves around us and our insights, making ourselves gods by claiming and naming life according to our vision and definition; or we will believe all outside ourselves is valid and real, while we are unreal and less than whole.

The reflected life lived in isolation will produce only "my story" and perhaps not even that, for it will be only "my view" of "my story" at a particular moment, in a particular mood. To be part of educational ministry, journal keeping needs to take place within the Christian community. We experience life as individuals, but we continue to hold that experience, by faith, as part of the new creation, the church.

Everything need not be shared with all the brothers and sisters in the church. At times each of us will need to say, "I." The God who formed me in my mother's womb, who knows my inmost thoughts, who counts every hair on my head, has pronounced me whole. I do not need to wait until I find a friend in order to share myself. I do not need people, as though being alone were incomplete. Dietrich Bonhoeffer in *Life Together* says, "Let the person who cannot be alone beware of community." [2]

186

Yet I carry with me, into my places alone, the brothers and sisters in the faith. Bonhoeffer also says, "Let the one who is not in community, beware of being alone." [3]

In my places apart, God places around me the lives of all the Christians through the centuries and the cares and joys of Christians around the world today.

"I am alone; I am whole; I am loved; I am complete in Christ," we can say. At the same time, the wholeness of the body of Christ is a living reality, bringing us comfort and challenging us, enabling each of us to be alone and thrusting us out again into the world.

There is another way of looking at reflected experience as an important way of doing theology. Just as the insurance agent could "go on without me" when his information was more than I could absorb, so I can easily let the church go on without me. The Bible remains on the shelf; the liturgy moves along while my body remains in the pew, but my mind has gone home. Committees and classes meet, but I am not present. But I cannot so easily leave my self.

If the self has been engaged all along (if not only sitting in class, book reading, test taking, but also life and experience, walking and sleeping and thinking have been the fabric of religious life), that self in relation to God and God's world and people will have to be dealt with. Some people call that spiritual formation.

To minister to the whole individual within the Christian community is to help that person adopt means to know the self in response to God's revelation in communion with the body of Christ.

Journal keeping at any age

As the child begins to know the self as separate from the mother, an important process of recognition and claiming begins: The child says, "My hand," "My foot." Early Sunday school activities include drawing pictures of "me" and "my family."

Much of this work must be done by the developing child personally. But even at this age, caring adults can aid the development of the reflective process. Studies of children's language development have shown that vocabulary and sentence construction develop best, not when the child is left to play alone, not when speech patterns are "corrected," not even when an adult imitates the child's speech with expansion (*Child:* "Dog brown." *Adult:* "The dog is brown."). The child's speech develops best when an attentive adult converses meaningfully about what the child says, providing words and meanings related to, but not the same as, the child has said (*Child:* "Kitty pretty." *Adult:* "I enjoy looking at the kitty, too.").[4]

Preschool and kindergarten

Some preschool and kindergarten classes provide children with journals. First the children draw pictures of their day. When one-on-one work is possible, a child and a teacher sit and talk about the child's day, including feelings as well as activities. The teacher may ask, "Do you want me to write for you?" The teacher writes the child's daily dictation into the journal. Unfortunately, in our education system, in not too many years, the student is asking the teacher, "What do you want me to write for you?"

At the stage when a child can write for himself, the journal can be dialogical, a conversation between the child and the teacher as trusted friend. A wise teacher will treat that trust with respect.

A sample journal from public school:

June 13: Today I am back from my trip.

Teacher's response: "How did you enjoy your trip? What did you especially like?"

June 16: Today I planted my bean's.

Teacher's response: (The teacher did not at this time correct the use of the apostrophe rather than the plural, but encouraged curiosity.) "How long do you think it will take before they start growing?"

June 18: Today my bean is coming out of the ground.

Teacher's response: "Soon it will be tall."

Middle and upper elementary

During the middle and upper elementary years, when children are ready for skill-building, child and teacher are more apt to turn their attention to proper spelling and grammar than to reflection. Although a 10-year-old may be intrigued with learning the names of dinosaurs or baseball players, the developing self still needs time and space to be alone and to think. What happens when a best friend moves away? What happens when parents fight? Does a child sleep well at night when one of those parents keeps a packed suitcase at the bottom of the stairs? The child needs to be able to feel and to articulate those emotions to begin to make sense out of reality.

This is an important time for journal keeping. Unfortunately, many of our children soon learn to fill their days to the brim, so that there are no interludes in which to reflect and remember, to wish and to dream.

The Christian community, which is a reflecting community, will encourage its children to become reflecting people, pondering the wonders of a creator God, growing in the sure faith and in the constant love of the God who never moves away, who doesn't keep a suitcase packed

189

ready to move out on us. A child may think, "This is not just *my* God, but the God of mom and dad and Mrs. Jones and Mr. Swenson." As the child learns to name the constellations in the summer sky, she realizes, "The God who created these stars is my God."

Is this the beginning of meditation? In a trusting relationship, in moments of sitting in a quiet place, in moments of writing in a journal, the child can dare to be honest: "I lied when I told the teacher I had my assignment done but left it at home," or "I shouldn't have told Sarah's mother that Sarah was the one who talked us into going to the store; now Sarah can't ride her bike for two days." The child may even begin to face the harmful consequences of self-protecting actions and to think about them. Is this the beginning of contrition and repentance?

How different from the "I didn't do it" litany children recite so easily. How much more real than the obligatory confession, "Okay, I'm sorry." How different from merely learning *about* the words *meditation, contrition,* and *repentance.*

Adolescence

As the child grows to adolescence and the search for identity begins in earnest, the reflective processes sharpen. The young person now is able to analyze and deal with situations not concretely before him. This ability to consider many possible solutions to a problem, combined with a need to find oneself as well as new ways of being together with people, makes adolescence a right time for journal keeping.

Given the question, "Why is the boy in the picture crying?" a young child might simply say, "His mother spanked him." The child would be satisfied with this first response and would not have thought of others. In con-

190

trast, the adolescent, posed the same question, would generate a number of hypotheses: "The boy might not have been able to find his mother; he might have been spanked; he could have hurt himself; he might not have been allowed to watch television; his mother might have scolded him because he lost his lunch." [5]

Teenagers have a hard time understanding themselves. David Ellkind says: "The adolescent is himself and assumes that other people are as obsessed with his behavior and appearance as he is." [6] A time for inner growth is essential if the changing self and widening world views are to coexist.

The teenager often plays to an imaginary audience. In fact, the whole world is *not* watching to see if Joe washed his hair, made the team, or got a date. But he imagines they are watching. A time for reflection, being alone to think and write about himself, might seem to feed this egocentric urge; on the contrary, it might help him focus the self-concern, clarify alternatives, and make decisions on his own. The alternative is to be bombarded with possibilities, ideas, world views, and not bring them into harmony with the emerging self. In this case the adolescent merely acts in response to a message from an advertiser or peer.

> The cognitive ability which enables an adolescent to conceive of and consider many alternative solutions to a problem helps her to solve complicated problems in math and science, but it doesn't necessarily help her in more practical situations. For example, a young adolescent may think of a number of ways to spend the summer; she could go to camp or summer school, do odd jobs, visit relatives in another state or stay home and just "hang around." But because she lacks experience in making decisions and doesn't really understand what the various alternatives involve, she either

> depends on her parents to make the decision for her,
> or she stays home, not really because she wants to, but
> because she can't decide what else to do.[7]

This is a time when writing for oneself alone is important. A Christian teacher should read a student's journal only if asked. If a journal is to be used in a junior or senior high Bible class, the teacher might introduce the concept, provide journal notebooks, and simply invite students to use them. Or the teacher might share some of his own personal journal entries, therefore modeling the effective use in the teacher's own life.

This is also a time when a significant adult relationship can be an important, cherished thing. The teacher might ask for a few journal entries to be handed in, but leave the selection of entries to the student. With encouraging, accepting responses from the teacher, the student's trust might soon be gained.

The student might test out the teacher, writing shocking things to tempt the teacher to "tell" or to reject. Or, more likely, the student may at first write carefully, saying only "acceptable" things. But in time, as the student learns that the teacher will not share the journal entries with other teachers, relatives, pastor, or parents, nor read them aloud in class, the student might be willing to share more and deeper thoughts as well.

The Bible class or youth group can be a place to discuss mutual ministry of peers. Sharing of journals with peers might seem easier than with teacher, but actually it is not, for the fluctuating friendships of teen years are as often the subject of journals as the place to confidently share them. To make a covenant with a person to be someone with whom to share one's journal is a serious responsibility: "The more deep things we share with each other, the less we want [those things] talked about elsewhere. The only way to have people trust us is to be trustworthy . . . there is probably nothing that can blow a growing relationship faster than a broken confidence." [8]

On our own we constantly need to use one another to build our own self worth. Knowing that my worth is from God and that I am free in Christ to become a person for others, I no longer need to "tell" in order either to preserve or to build my own identity and self-worth. I can say, "I am enough of a person to tell this to." And I can add, "My friend in Christ is free enough to be my confidant, and I am free enough to be a friend."

Junior and senior high years are a good time to introduce journal keeping with the Psalms. A number of years ago among my confirmands was a bright, respectful young man who was unhappy in school. Most of the time Bob couldn't stand his classmates, who probably had little affection for him or his interests. As part of the class, I had each person "mark the Psalms" in order to use the Psalter as a monthly prayer book (see Appendix, p. 221). Each student was then to pray the Psalms over the course of the month. They were also to memorize some verses— the number and choice were left to them—from a psalm which really seemed to speak to them and which they could claim as their own, one which was therefore worth committing to memory. They could then come the next week, sharing their selection with me. Bob's favorite psalms were the vengeance psalms: 68, 88, 94, and 35, with verses like this one: "Contend, O Lord, with those who contend with me; fight against those who fight against me."

In the psalmist he found another person of God who shared his anger, his frustration. Those were his real, honest feelings, even though they might seem misdirected

193

or unfitting. That was where Bob was, and he could bring his self to God and leave those feelings there.

Those years of confirmation were important for Bob, and for me and the class, although he did not at that time develop close peer relationships. Later when I saw Bob again after he had completed his first year of college, I asked him, "How did you like it? I don't want to know how you did: I'm sure you did fine. How did you like it?"

He answered, "I just loved it." He had finally found himself and peers; he and they fit. But his God had been with him all along.

Adults

Adults will also find journal keeping with the Psalms a good way of reflecting and praying. I sometimes say to a group of adults, "Close your eyes and think back over the past week. What moods have you been in? What strong emotions have you felt?" After a few moments for them to relive those emotions, they show with a nod, "Yes, indeed, we have experienced many feelings this past week."

We may then take a few minutes to share these feelings with the person next to us. All those feelings are recorded in the Psalms. Then as a group we will read some psalms, perhaps Psalm 30: "Weeping may spend the night, but joy comes in the morning." As a group we might then read some psalms back and forth by whole or half verses, or sing them. As we go apart from each other, we might also read the Psalms at home, as part of personal journal keeping.

Adults need to know it is acceptable to have the strong feelings they have and that it is permissible to write about them. The beginning journal writer will often make the diary a polite logging of the day's events, using a formal style she would not even use in casual conversation. Such polite conversation discourages one from becoming better acquainted, even with oneself.

A person needs a quiet place, a special time. He needs a place to write where he will be uninterrupted. The adult also needs to set himself free from baggage he carried with him from a seventh-grade teacher's judgments about his spelling errors, messy papers, and incomplete sentences.

There may already be journal writers in the congregation. I was surprised to talk with a woman who had recently retired from a job of working with special children in a state school. She told me of her plans for retirement:

> I want to have time to write. I have 13 journals in which I wrote about my work. I've been married 45 years, and sometimes I go back and read the things I wrote when my children were growing up. I can hardly believe I felt as I did when I wrote those days, but I did. That's how I felt, and I understand it now.

I had often marveled at this woman's inner strength, her quiet resolution, the initiative she showed in beginning a class at church for retarded young adults. Her journal writing, her honest, reflective meditation were ongoing means of Christian growth, and she speaks convincingly of God's strength in her life.

In *Journal for Life* George Simon writes:

> Religious growth depends to a great degree on the individual's facility at getting in touch with the intensity, the succession and the flow of personal experience . . . keeping a journal creates an accessible record of the dialogue of the inner person and outer world and [is therefore] a means of spiritual development.[9]

> Communicating your own experiences to yourself in this way is the surest way to get meaning out of them. So many people say that their lives are meaningless

and that they feel worthless. This is precisely because
they actually throw their lives away by alienating
their own experience and feelings.[10]

Journal keeping—reflection upon one's life and learning from that reflection—is hard, but refreshing work.
It requires discipline, and it assumes that individual takes
responsibility for her own learning.

Progoff's intensive journal

Ira Progoff's journal workshops across this country
have introduced many to a process which relates the outer
journey of daily events with the inner journey. He believes that the self has more vitality and open-ended,
health-giving properties than most people realize.

In the workshop people record not only a daily log, but
a period log, noting the particular periods in their lives
which had special meaning. Participants also write about
the "stepping-stones" of their lives and carry on "dialogs"
with persons, events, and works of those periods.

Progoff encourages us to engage in such dialogues in
nonjudgmental ways, without interpreting or analyzing.
He claims that the self will be its own corrective. In using
the journal with many ages, Progoff trusts the method.
People attend the workshops together, but their work is
individual. "This . . . solitary work we cannot do alone,"
Progoff says.[11] The response is not from a trusted friend
or teacher, but from sections of one's own journal.

Progoff has found that continuous use of the journal
has a self-propelling effect. The goal is to build an inner
perspective on one's own life. "Retracing our stepping-stones has the effect of marking off the lines of continuity

196

in our development. We can see where we are, and we can follow the succession of events by which we came to the present situation in our life."[12]

Progoff says that the stepping-stones of our spiritual life in all its forms and phases can be recalled and provide us with new possibilities of meaning as well. Past Sunday school classes, experiences of Christian community, the riches of the Scriptures which were implanted years before may open new possibilities for us, for many have been carried silently inside of us year after year. Although we cannot go back and relive a decision made at a cross-road years before, there are possibilities of life still present and available to us and it is these that are valuable to explore.

> Considering the unlived potentials of our life is reminiscent of an event that took place in the nineteenth century when an ancient Egyptian tomb was opened. In that tomb a portion of a tree was found, and imbedded in the wood was a seed. The scientists involved in the expedition planted the seed out of curiosity, merely to see if anything would happen. Behold, after three thousand years the seed grew! It had missed its chance to grow in ancient Egypt, but its strength of life had remained intact, dormant and waiting for its next opportunity.[13]

We have the promise that God's seed, once planted, will bear fruit, "For as the rain and the snow come down from heaven . . . , giving seed to the sower and bread to the eater, so shall my word be . . . ; it shall not return to me empty" (Isa. 55:10-11).

The private journey of journal keeping fosters deep growth. Working with our present events and reflections and dreams, as well as working with the past, provides opportunity for continuous growth for the individual, and thereby for the community.

There are cultures in which the family takes time in the morning to share the dreams of each member the previous night. There are places, rare as they may seem today, in our present culture where families still sit on front porches or back patios and reflect and hope together. The Christian family needs to create time and ways to share their common history and dream their common future. The members of a Christian community, having been creatively alone, have much more to bring to each other. And so, in one more way, the Christian community is able to teach and learn from one another.

Notes

Chapter 1   Presentation

1. Two good books on storytelling are Ruth Sawyer, *The Way of the Storyteller*, Viking Press, 1942, 1962, and Wallace Hildick, *Thirteen Types of Narrative*, Clarkson N. Potter, 1970.

Chapter 2   Worshiping Community

1. Dietrich Bonhoeffer, *Life Together*, Harper & Row, 1954, pp. 26-27.

Chapter 3   Discussion

1. For helpful guidelines for asking questions, see Donald L. Griggs, *Teaching Teachers to Teach*, Abingdon, 1974, p. 75.

2. Henri Nouwen, *Creative Ministry*, Doubleday, 1978, p. 6.

3. Thomas Gordon, *Teacher Effectiveness Training*, Peter H. Wyden, 1974, pp. 87-88.

Chapter 4 Inductive Study

1. John Holt, *How Children Fail*, Dell, 1964, p. 210.

2. Holt, pp. 207-208.

3. See Barry J. Wadsworth, *Piaget's Theory of Cognitive Development*, David McKay Co., 1974, and Mary M. Wilcox, *Developmental Journey: A Guide to the Development of Logical and Moral Reasoning and Social Perspective*, Abingdon, 1979.

4. Philip E. Pederson, ed., *What Does This Mean? Luther's Catechisms Today*, Augsburg, 1976, pp. 31-32.

5. Roland H. Bainton, *The Church of Our Fathers*, Charles Scribner's Sons, 1941, p. 47.

6. Pederson, p. 23.

7. Maria Louisa Charlesworth, *Ministering Children*, American Tract Society, Circa 1850, preface.

8. *Lutheran Book of Worship*, Augsburg, 1978, "Holy Baptism," p. 121.

9. Thomas Droege, *Self-Realization and Faith: Beginning and Becoming in Relation to God*, Lutheran Education Association, 1978, pp. 1-6.

10. Ronald Goldman, *Readiness for Religion*, Seabury, 1965, p. 99.

11. Goldman, p. 71.

12. Gerard Pottebaum, *The Praise Parade: Psalm 150*, George A. Pflaum, Inc., 1967; the *Little People's Paperbacks* series is now available from Seabury, New York.

13. See *Education Resources for the Congregation, 1983-84*, Augsburg, 1983, pp. 8, 25, 33 for such curriculum enrichment resources as *How the Bible Came to Us, How Bible People Lived,* and for teachers, *Many Words, One Word,* and *The Bible and Our Faith*.

Chapter 5 Individualized Learning

1. Charles E. Silberman, ed., *The Open Classroom Reader*, Random House, 1973, pp. 5-6.

2. Silberman, p. 39.

3. Silberman, pp. 11-12.

4. John M. Larsen, "Learning Space for a Learning Community," in John Westerhoff, ed., *A Colloquy on Christian Education,* Pilgrim Press, 1972, p. 113.

5. Mary E. and Andrew Jensen, *Confirmation Workshop Manual,* Christian Education Media, 1975, p. 53.

6. Allan Tough, *The Adult's Learning Projects,* 2nd ed., Learning Concepts, 1979. Tough assesses that about 70% of all adults' learning projects are planned by the learner.

Chapter 6 Confrontation and Clarification

1. Suzanne De Dietrich, *The Witnessing Community,* Westminster, 1958, p. 16.

2. Louis E. Raths, Merrill Harmin, and Sidney Simon, *Values and Teaching,* Charles E. Merrill, 1966, p. 30.

3. For examples of teaching at the facts level, the concepts level, and the values level, see Merrill Harmin, Howard Kirschenbaum, and Sidney Simon, *Clarifying Values Through Subject Matter,* Winston, 1973.

4. Richard Curwin and Geri Curwin, *Developing Individual Values in the Classroom,* Learning Handbooks Series, 1974, p. 8.

5. Lecture by Sidney Simon, University of Dubuque, Dubuque, Iowa, Sept. 6, 1980.

6. Donald Bossart, *Creative Conflict in Religious Education and Church Administration,* Religious Education Press, 1980.

7. Bossart, pp. 255-257.

Chapter 7 Experiential Learning

1 Letty M. Russell, *Christian Education in Mission,* Westminster, 1967, p. 25.

2. James D. and Evelyn Eaton Whitehead, *Method in Ministry:*

Theological Reflection and Christian Ministry, Seabury, 1980, pp. 11-26.

3. John Westerhoff, "Contemporary Spirituality: Revelation Myth and Ritual," in Gloria Durka and Joanmarie Smith, eds., *Aesthetic Dimensions of Religious Education*, Paulist, 1979, pp. 13-27.

4. Robert E. Horn, *The Guide to Simulations/Games for Education and Training*, vols. 1-2, Didache Systems, Inc., Box 457, Cranford, N.J. 07016.

5. J. William Pfeiffer and John E. Jones, University Associates Publishers and Consultants, Inc., 8517 Production Avenue, P.O. Box 26240, San Diego, Calif. 92126.

6. Richard Reichert, *Simulation Games for Religious Education*, John Knox, 1977, pp. 2-3.

7. Reichert, p. 16.

8. Gabriel Moran, "Work, Leisure, and Religious Education," in *Religious Education*, March-April, 1979, p. 160.

9. Herb Brokering, *Wholly Holy*, Lutheran Education Association, 1976, p. 32.

10. Norma Everist, *Religions of the World*, Ages 13-18, Pflaum, 1979, p. 9.

Chapter 8   Journal Keeping

1. George F. Simons, *Journal for Life: Discovering Faith and Values Through Journal Keeping*, Part 2, Foundation for Adult Catechetical Teaching Aids, 1977, p. 2.

2. Dietrich Bonhoeffer, *Life Together*, Harper & Row, 1954, p. 77.

3. Bonhoeffer, p. 77.

4. Lisa Smith, *Human Development, 2½ to 6 Years*, filmstrip, Concept Media, Inc., 1977, Program 3, "Language Development," Instructor's Manual, pp. 40-44.

5. Lisa Smith, *Human Development, The Adolescent Years*,

12-16, filmstrip, Concept Media, Inc., 1977, Program 4, Part 1, "Cognitive Development," Instructor's Manual, p. 53.

6. David Elkind, "Egocentrism in Adolescence," in *Child Development*, Vol. 8, p. 1030.

7. Lisa Smith, *Human Development, The Adolescent Years, 12-16*, filmstrip, Concept Media, Inc., 1977, Program 5, Part 2, "Cognitive Development," Instructor's Manual, p. 69.

8. Kenneth Fletcher and others, *Extend: Youth Reaching Youth*, Augsburg, 1974, pp. 47-48.

9. George Simons, *Journal of Life*, Part 1, p. 7.

10. Simons, p. 3.

11. Ira Progoff, *At A Journal Workshop: The Basic Text and Guide for Using the Intensive Journal*, Dialogue House Library, 1975, p. 52.

12. Progoff, p. 134.

13. Progoff, p. 135.

For Further Reading

Educational ministry in general

Freire, Paulo. *Pedagogy of the Oppressed.* Transl. by Myra Bergman Ramos. New York: Herder and Herder, 1970.

Groome, Thomas. *Christian Religious Education.* San Francisco: Harper and Row, 1982.

Harris, Maria. *Portrait of Youth Ministry.* New York: Paulist, 1981.

Joyce, Bruce and Weil, Marsha. *Models of Teaching.* Englewood Cliffs, N.J.: Prentice-Hall, Inc., 1972.

Lema, Anza A. *Pedagogical and Theological Presuppositions of Education.* Hong Kong: Lutheran Southeast Asia Christian Curricula Committee—Lutheran World Federation, 1977.

McKenzie, Leon. *The Religious Education of Adults.* Birmingham, Ala.: Religious Education Press, 1982.

Miller, Randolph Crump. *The Theory of Christian Education Practices: How Theology Affects Christian Education*. Birmingham, Ala.: Religious Education Press, 1980.

O'Hare, Padraic, ed. *Tradition and Transformation in Religious Education*. Birmingham, Ala.: Religious Educaton Press, 1979.

Russell, Letty M. *Christian Education in Mission*. Philadelphia: Westminster, 1967.

Warford, Malcolm L. *The Necessary Illusion*. Philadelphia: United Church Press, 1976.

Westerhoff, John, ed. *A Colloquy on Christian Education*. New York: Pilgrim Press, 1972.

Westerhoff, John, ed. *Who Are We? The Quest for a Religious Education*. Birmingham, Ala.: Religious Education Press, 1978.

Westerhoff, John. *Will Our Children Have Faith?* New York: Seabury, 1976.

Presentation

Bettelheim, Bruno. *The Uses of Enchantment: The Meaning and Importance of Fairy Tales*. New York: Vintage Books, 1977.

Cohen, Barbara. *The Binding of Isaac*. New York: Lothrop, Lee & Shepard Co., 1978.

Dunne, John S. *Time and Myth: A Meditation on Storytelling as an Exploration of Life and Death*. Notre Dame: University of Notre Dame Press, 1975.

Everist, Norma and Rowland II, Robert. *A Children's Life of Jesus*. Mark, Luke-Acts Audio Visual Program,

(24 filmstrips). Mystic, Conn.: Twenty-third Publications, 1982.

Hildick, Wallace. *Thirteen Types of Narrative.* New York: Clarkson N. Potter, 1970.

Sawyer, Ruth. *The Way of the Storyteller.* New York: Viking Press, 1942, 1962.

Worshiping community

Abernethy, William. *A New Look for Sunday Morning.* Nashville: Abingdon, 1975.

Arms, Myron, and Denman, David. *Touching the World.* New York: Charles Scribner's Sons, 1975.

Bonhoeffer, Dietrich. *Life Together.* New York: Harper and Row, 1954.

Bushnell, Horace. *Christian Nurture.* Forge Village, Mass.: Murray Printing Company, 1883; reprinted New Haven: Yale University Press, 1967; also Grand Rapids, Michigan: Baker Book House, 1979.

De Dietrich, Suzanne. *The Witnessing Community.* Philadelphia: Westminster, 1958.

Gobbel, Roger A. and Huber, Phillip C. *Creative Designs with Children at Worship.* Atlanta: John Knox, 1981.

Griggs, Donald and Griggs, Patricia. *Generations Learning Together.* Nashville: Abingdon, 1976.

Palmer, Parker J. *The Company of Strangers.* New York: Crossroad, 1981.

Russell, Letty M. *Growth in Partnership.* Philadelphia: Westminster, 1981.

Sawin, Margaret M. *Family Enrichment with Family Clusters.* Valley Forge, Pa.: Judson, 1979.

Wynn, J. C. *Christian Education for Liberation and Other Upsetting Ideas.* Nashville: Abingdon, 1977.

Discussion

Bowman, Jr., Locke. *Teaching Today: The Church's First Ministry.* Philadelphia: Westminster, 1980.

Bush, John H. and Jones, Sandy. *Developing the Art of Discussion.* Valley Forge, Pa.: Judson, 1977.

Duska, Ronald and Whelan, Mariellen. *Moral Development: A Guide to Piaget and Kohlberg.* New York: Paulist, 1975.

Everist, Burton L. *The Christian Family Craft Book.* Wilton, Conn.: Morehouse-Barlow Co., 1978.

Galbraith, Ronald E. and Jones, Thomas M. *Moral Reasoning: A Teaching Handbook for Adopting Kohlberg to the Classroom.* Anoka, Minn.: Greenhaven Press, Inc., 1976.

Gordon, Thomas. *Teacher Effectiveness Training.* New York: Peter H. Wyden, 1974.

Griggs, Donald L. *Teaching Teachers to Teach.* Nashville: Abingdon, 1974.

Hunter, David R. *Christian Education as Engagement.* New York: Seabury, 1963.

Nouwen, Henri J. M. *Creative Ministry.* Garden City, N.Y.: Image Books, Doubleday, 1978.

Rogers, Donald B. *In Praise of Learning.* Nashville: Abingdon, 1980.

Inductive study

Bainton, Roland H. *The Church of Our Fathers.* New York: Charles Scribner's Sons, 1941.

Browning, Robert L. and Foster, Charles R. *Ways the Bible Comes Alive.* Nashville: Abingdon, 1975 (four cassettes, resource book, and learner book).

Cully, Iris. *Christian Child Development.* San Francisco: Harper and Row, 1979.

Droege, Thomas. *Self-Realization and Faith: Beginning and Becoming in Relation to God.* Chicago: Lutheran Education Association, 1978.

Fowler, James. *Stages of Faith: The Psychology of Human Development and the Quest for Meaning.* San Francisco: Harper and Row, 1981.

Furnish, Dorothy Jean. *Exploring the Bible with Children.* Nashville: Abingdon, 1975.

Goldman, Ronald. *Readiness for Religion.* New York: Seabury, 1965.

Griggs, Donald L. *Twenty New Ways of Teaching the Bible.* Nashville: Abingdon, 1977.

Holt, John. *How Children Fail.* New York: Dell Publishing Co., 1964.

Smith, Lisa. *Human Development, The Adolescent Years, 12-16,* and *2½ to 6 Years* (filmstrip series). Costa Mesa, Calif.: Concept Media, Inc., 1977.

Wilcox, Mary. *Developmental Journey: A Guide to the Development of Logical and Moral Reasoning and Social Perspective.* Nashville: Abingdon, 1979.

Individualized learning

Duckert, Mary. *Open Education Goes to Church.* Philadelphia: Westminster, 1976.

Gray, David and Elizabeth. *Children of Joy: Raising Your Own Home-Grown Christians*. Branford, Conn.: Readers Press, Inc., 1975.

Silberman, Charles E., ed. *The Open Classroom Reader*. New York: Random House, 1973.

Taylor, Joy. *Organizing the Open Classroom*. New York: Schocken Books, 1971.

Tough, Allen. *The Adult's Learning Projects*. Second Edition. Toronto, Ontario: Learning Concepts, 1979.

Confrontation and clarification

Blum, Virgil C. *Education: Freedom and Competition*. Chicago: Argus Communications Co., 1967.

Bossart, Donald. *Creative Conflict in Religious Education and Church Administration*. Birmingham, Ala.: Religious Education Press, 1980.

Dittes, James E. *When the People Say No*. San Francisco: Harper and Row, 1979.

Harmin, Merrill, Kirschenbaum, and Simon. *Clarifying Values Through Subject Matter*. Minneapolis: Winston, 1973.

Larson, Roland S. and Larson, Doris E. *Values and Faith: Value Clarifying Exercises for Family and Church Groups*. Minneapolis: Winston, 1976.

Raths, Louis E., Harmin, Merrill, and Simon, Sidney B. *Values and Teaching*. Columbus: Charles E. Merrill, 1966.

Simon, Sidney B., Howe, Leland W., and Krischenbaum, Howard. *Values Clarification*. New York: Hart Publishing Co. Inc., 1972.

Experiential learning

Brokering, Herbert. *Wholly Holy*. River Forest, Ill.: Lutheran Education Association, 1976.

Burger, Isabel B. *Creative Drama in Religious Education*. Wilton, Conn.: Morehouse-Barlow Co., 1977.

Carson, Rachel. *The Sense of Wonder*. New York: Harper and Row, 1956.

Durka, Gloria and Smith, Joanmarie, eds. *Aesthetic Dimensions of Religious Education*. New York: Paulist, 1979.

Durland, Frances Caldwell. *Creative Dramatics for Children*. Kent, Ohio: Kent State University Press, 1975.

Everist, Norma. *Religions of the World, Ages 13-18*. Dayton, Ohio: Pflaum, 1979.

Hendrix, John and Hendrix, Lela. *Experiential Education: X-ED*. Nashville: Abingdon, 1975.

Layman, James E. *Using Case Studies in Church Education*. Scottsdale, Ariz.: National Teacher Education Project, 1977.

Mattox, Beverly A. *Getting It Together: Dilemmas for the Classroom*. San Diego, Calif.: Pennant Press, 1975.

Miller, Donald E., Snyder, Graydon F., and Neff, Robert W. *Using Biblical Simulation*. Valley Forge, Pa.: Judson, 1975.

Moran, Gabriel. *Education Toward Adulthood: Religion and Lifelong Learning*. New York: Paulist, 1979.

Pinkerton, Todd. *Breaking Communication Barriers with Roleplay*. Atlanta, Ga.: John Knox, 1976.

Reichert, Richard. *Simulation Games for Religious Education*. Atlanta: John Knox, 1977.

Stenzel, Anne K. and Feeney, Helen M. *Learning by the Case Method*. New York: Seabury, 1970.

Tobey, Kathrene M. *Learning and Teaching Through the Senses*. Philadelphia: Westminster, 1970.

Ward, Colin. *The Child of the City*. New York: Pantheon Books, 1978.

Journal keeping

Brooke, Avery. *Hidden in Plain Sight: The Practice of Christian Meditation*. New York: Seabury, 1978.

Fader, Daniel N. and Shaevitz, Morton H. *Hooked on Books*. New York: Berkley Publishing Corp., 1966.

Fletcher, Kenneth R., Norem-Hebeisen, Johnson, and Underwager, Ralph. *Extend: Youth Reaching Youth*. Minneapolis: Augsburg, 1974.

Klug, Ronald. *How to Keep a Spiritual Journal*. Nashville: Thomas Nelson, 1982.

Progoff, Ira. *At a Journal Workshop: The Basic Text and Guide for Using the Intensive Journal*. New York: Dialogue House Library, 1975.

Simons, George F. *Journal for Life: Discovering Faith and Values Through Journal Keeping*. Chicago: Foundation for Adult Catechetical Teaching Aids, 1975.

Appendix 1

Case Studies

The following are two sample case studies for use with adult classes. They might also be used as an educational component of a church council meeting, outreach workshop, lay-ministry committee or wherever vicarious experiential learning would be helpful as adults grow in understanding and skills. Through dealing objectively with a situation other than their own, the learners are able to surface and deal with issues, and thereby grow in *skills* of dealing with issues more easily and clearly than when embroiled in their own existential conflict.

The following are actual situations, with names changed. The issues beneath the situation occur, in varying form, in any congregation. Each person is provided a case study to read ahead of the discussion period. The leader continues with open-ended questions: (Use of a chalkboard to record comments is helpful.)

1. What are the issues you see here?
2. Who are the people involved and what do we know about them?
3. What are the deeper issues, the ministry issues?
4. What are the options for decision and action?

The outcome of the case study is not nearly as important as the discussion of issues and the exercise of seeing the question through the eyes of various people. The participants are then encouraged to think more deeply about theological issues underlying this problem, the basic questions which each congregation faces, even though the outward problems might appear different. Participants need not speculate or add, "Well, in our congregation it was like. . . ." They rather are encouraged to discuss on the basis of the situation presented, the information actually known through the case study. The case studies are open-ended; the outcome is uncertain so that participants will not be faced with agreeing or disagreeing, but will ascertain issues and options.

At first, the case-study method may be new and therefore a bit slow, but soon the adults will be adding many insights. They will discover that as a group they discern many more facets of a situation than any one person could alone. Allow about an hour for case-study discussion.

Case 1: Mutual Ministry at Community of Faith

The celebration of the Festival of the Resurrection was over, but the members of Community of Faith were living in the afterglow, overflowing with enthusiasm to communicate the faith with renewed vigor.

Community was an exciting place to be. Things were

on the upswing. The new pastor had been on the job for four weeks now. The intern, who had been on his own during the seven-month vacancy, had done an outstanding job of involving more people in the ministry of the church than ever before. Programs had been going great, and more people had joined the church in those past seven months than in the whole previous year.

Emily, a housewife and mother of two grown sons, had been a member of Community for the past 10 years, and for two years had headed up the Community Church Women evangelism calling program. The program had been going well with eight teams of women going out on evangelism calls regularly. Emily referred to this type of calling as "soft calls." The women would obtain the names of all the newcomers to the suburb and would pay a visit to the homes. During these visits they would share pertinent information about the area, tell the families about the community-wide program of caring sponsored by the area Christian churches, and then invite the families to worship at Community. They would also invite the families to attend a "Welcome Tea" sponsored by the women as an opportunity for the newcomers to get together and meet people in a hospitable environment. Emily loved being a part of this vital program of caring for people.

Jane, Emily's calling partner, was a young housewife and mother of four who exuded hospitality. Jane was a good conversationalist who loved meeting people. It was her responsibility to keep accurate records of the visits made. She would write summary paragraphs about each visit when the teams came back to the church after their calls. When she had written these reports she would share the information with the pastor to aid him in his visits.

On Tuesday morning Emily and Jane had an appointment with the new pastor to communicate to him the willingness of the women to continue with this program and to assist him in what ever ways they could. The Community Church Women was anxious to be a part of the outreach ministry of the church and were seeking his direction.

Pastor Solo listened as they shared their enthusiasm about the calling program, paused a moment, and then replied, "There really isn't any need for you to continue that type of calling program now. The intern and I will be doing all the evangelism calling from now on. You are welcome to go along with one of us as we make our visits, but we will be responsible for the calls and the follow-up."

Emily and Jane left the office a few moments later. Within a few short months the evangelism calling program of the Community Church Women was a thing of the past.

Three years later the evangelism program at Community was essentially the responsibility of each year's intern. When Intern Eve arrived and requested assistance in evangelism calling, there was a distinct hesitancy on the part of the members to become involved in the calling program. When she asked Emily why people were hesitant, Emily responded, "The evangelism calling program at Community is the responsibility of the professionals; lay people aren't equipped for that phase of ministry."

Eve experienced a deep sense of sadness.

Case 2: To whom will they listen?

Pastor Larson entered the office of the new assistant pastor, Jim Martin and asked, "Are you ready to assist at your first funeral?" He continued by saying this would be an especially difficult funeral because a 16-year-old member of the congregation had been murdered in an Hispanic-white gang confrontation.

The day of the funeral was tense with threats of more violence. The funeral took place with no incident except for some graffiti and bottle throwing at the church that evening. As a result of the threats of violence, it was decided that the church must look at its mission. The pastor decided that the best place for this discussion to take place would be at the next council meeting.

The council meeting began on time. After the opening prayer the group quickly went through the secretary's, treasurer's and committee reports. Next on the agenda was the pastor's report. Pastor Larson began, "I am sure that we are all aware of the events of the last few weeks. The tragic death of Tony, the vandalism to our property, and threats of more violence. Concordia has been called a white island in the midst of a Hispanic community. I think it only fair that you be aware of what is happening."

A hush fell over the council as the words "white island" sunk in.

Ed, a charter member who is now retired, was the first to speak. "I have been here 25 years. We have always worshiped on this corner and if they consider us a white island, that's their problem, not ours."

Marie, who has always been very visible in the church and community, was next to speak. "I am sure that we are all aware of the changes that have been happening in our community. Fifty percent of our community is Hispanic. We can no longer walk the streets without seeing many different people. It's time we open our eyes and reach out and invite these people in. We cannot exist as we have. We will die; our church will die; and I'm sure we don't want that."

Alf, a quiet, reserved gentleman of Norwegian heritage spoke up. "We have always been a white-German-Norwegian congregation. I see no reason that we should change because of a few Mexicans. They can come to us. Besides, aren't they Catholic? Let St. Vincent's have them."

Marie again spoke. "Most Hispanics are unchurched. This can be a prime opportunity for us to be God's people reaching out in the world."

The rest of the council sat quietly, including Mark, the brother of the boy who was killed. Finally Dennis, 33, and a bachelor, who is vice-president of the council, spoke up. "I like things the way they are. I see no reason to change. I suggest we move on to the next item on the agenda. We need money counters for November. Who will volunteer?

The next morning when the assistant pastor came in, Pastor Larson asked what he thought of the meeting. Pastor Martin responded that he had found it frustrating. "I didn't think the church was ready to face change, but sooner or later they will have to."

"Yes," Pastor Larson replied. "I'm afraid you are right. Somehow we have to address the issues. But I have been here too long and they won't listen." Silence descended on the office. Then Pastor Larson spoke again, "You're new. Maybe they would listen to you."

"I don't know," Jim replied, "I have been here only two months."

Pastor Larson went on, "You preach next Sunday. Why don't you try to address the Hispanic issue in your sermon."

Appendix 2

Fantasy

A group of adults who are teachers or preparing to be teachers might benefit from the following experiential learning through fantasy.

Having set a learning environment of trust and relaxation, the leader invites the participants to sit back and become comfortable, shutting out thoughts from the day.

"I invite you to close your eyes and to let your mind relax. Go back through the years to a time when you were a student in a classroom. (The leader might insert here: "It was an uncomfortable time," or, "It was an enjoyable time," or might leave it open-ended.) *Pause.*

Quietly, so as not to interrupt thoughts forming: "You are there with other students and the teacher. Whom do you see? Who is nearby? Where are you in the room? Who else is in the room?" *Pause.* "What's going on? What's happening? What are you doing? What are others doing?" *Pause.* "What are you feeling?"

During a long pause, perhaps three-four minutes, the leader watches participants' body language to see if they are still engrossed in their own mental images. Finally the leader says quietly, "You may stay where you are for a few minutes and, when you are ready, open your eyes and rejoin the group here."

Then, within 10 or 15 seconds, as people begin to open their eyes, the leader begins conversation. The tone should be quiet and affirming. The leader might invite the group to share their fantasies in pairs, assuring them that they can talk about it as much or as little as they wish. Almost always, people will share this fantasy with someone next to them. (If the group is small, the leader, addressing the whole group, might invite, "Is there anyone who would like to share where they went in their fantasy?") After 5-6 minutes the paired groups might join the larger group and share learnings with the group as a whole.

This fantasy is helpful in bringing to the surface experiences of long ago in relation to their roles of learner and teacher. They may have unexamined feelings such as "I remembered how it felt to be afraid when I didn't have my assignment done." Discussion afterward will no doubt move into negative and positive aspects of teaching, but the primary value of fantasy is the recovery of feelings. Such feelings must be handled with care and respect by the leader and the group. Allow time and opportunity later if such experiential education gives rise to further recollections the participants may want to talk about.

The Psalter as Prayer Book

The Psalms show us human being pouring out their fears, joys, anxieties, vengeance, thanksgiving to a God who has promised to hear. While reading one psalm or a part of a psalm is useful for devotion, a person may want to become familiar with the entire Psalter, journal keeping along the way.

Youth and adults can take on the challenge of reading the entire Psalter in one month using the following marking system in one's own Bible. The Bible thereby becomes a prayer book, with a specific section to read on a specific morning or evening of the month. As the Psalms are re-read, a person might come back again to a date in his past when that Psalm matched his own feelings.

The following marking system takes about 15 minutes, and could be done in class or alone. At Psalm 1, mark 1-M to indicate that the person on the first day of the month in the morning reads Psalms 1-4. At Psalm 5 mark 1-E.

On the evening of the first day of the month the person reads Psalm 5-8. If one begins reading the Psalms on February 11, one would read in the morning Psalms 58 and 59.

Mark the Psalms thus:

Psalm 1	1-M	Psalm 60	11-E	Psalm 107	22-M
Psalm 5	1-E	Psalm 64	12-M	Psalm 108	22-E
Psalm 9	2-M	Psalm 66	12-E	Psalm 112	23-M
Psalm 12	2-E	Psalm 69	13-M	Psalm 116	23-E
Psalm 18	3-M	Psalm 70	13-E	Psalm 119:1	24-M
Psalm 19	3-E	Psalm 73	14-M	Psalm 119:41	24-E
Psalm 23	4-M	Psalm 74	14-E	Psalm 119:89	25-M
Psalm 26	4-E	Psalm 77	15-M	Psalm 119:129	25-E
Psalm 31	5-M	Psalm 78	15-E	Psalm 120	26-M
Psalm 33	5-E	Psalm 79	16-M	Psalm 126	26-E
Psalm 35	6-M	Psalm 81	16-E	Psalm 133	27-M
Psalm 36	6-E	Psalm 84	17-M	Psalm 136	27-E
Psalm 38	7-M	Psalm 86	17-E	Psalm 140	28-M
Psalm 39	7-E	Psalm 89	18-M	Psalm 142	28-E
Psalm 42	8-M	Psalm 90	18-E	Psalm 144	29-M
Psalm 45	8-E	Psalm 93	19-M	Psalm 145	29-E
Psalm 49	9-M	Psalm 96	19-E	Psalm 146	30-M
Psalm 50	9-E	Psalm 101	20-M	Psalm 147	30-E
Psalm 52	10-M	Psalm 103	20-E	Psalm 148	31-M
Psalm 55	10-E	Psalm 105	21-M	Psalm 149	31-E
Psalm 58	11-M	Psalm 106	21-E		

In months with fewer than 31 days, days 30 and 31 are combined.

Not all of these psalms will pertain specifically to the individual's day. However, in the discipline of reading the entire Psalter, many possibilities for journal keeping with the Psalms will be opened up to the person.